IMPLEMENTING HOLISTIC GOVERNMENT

Joined-up action on the ground

David Wilkinson and Elaine Appelbee

The POLICY PRESS

DEMOS

In memory of the creative, innovative and inspirational leadership of Gordon Charles Moore (1928-98), doyen of local authority chief executives.

First published in Great Britain in 1999 by

The Policy Press
University of Bristol
34 Tyndall's Park Road
Bristol BS8 1PY
UK
Tel +44 (0)117 954 6800
Fax +44 (0)117 973 7308
E-mail tpp@bristol.ac.uk
www.policypress.org.uk

© The Policy Press 1999
Reprinted 2001

ISBN 1 86134 143 1

David Wilkinson is a partner in the consultancy network, Whole System Development and is based in Keighley, West Yorkshire (Tel 01535 680537).
Elaine Appelbee is the Bishop of Bradford's Officer for church in society and works from 168 Highfield Lane, Keighley, West Yorkshire.

Cover design by Qube Design Associates, Bristol.
Photographs used on front cover supplied by kind permission of the Touchstone Centre, Bradford and the authors.
Printed in Great Britain by Hobbs the Printers Ltd, Southampton.

Contents

Contents

Editorial preface

The Labour government's aims for a radical modernisation of Britain, and especially for a fundamental attack on the causes and consequences of poverty, crime and chronic unemployability, depend on its ability to make a reality of the idea of 'holistic government'. This notion – better known as 'joined-up thinking' and 'joined-up policy' – has become a soundbite and is in danger of being seen as a cliché with no substance. But it is at the heart of the government's ambitions to go down as a radical reforming administration.

Holistic government is about achieving substantially better outcomes across a wide range of policy areas in which we have become accustomed to fatalism and underperformance. Successive governments have failed to tackle deep-seated problems of poverty and all the associated ills known as 'social exclusion' on our worst council estates; they have presided over a steady decline in the performance of public transport systems; and they have failed to raise levels of educational attainment, environmental quality and health for the worst-off parts of society.

Overcoming the legacy of fatalism and low expectations about the scope for progress in these areas and actually achieving better outcomes on a large scale is not simply a matter of unlocking more public money or drawing up better legislation. It requires a cultural revolution in central and local government, and a new way of looking at policy design and implementation. This is what holistic government is about.

Why do we need this revolution? The key reason is that many costs are incurred, and many problems exacerbated, because of failures of coordination and communication between departments and agencies at central and local levels. The joined-up quality of problems – those experienced, say, by elderly people with no relatives to care for them, or by disaffected young people with poor local schools and troubled families – is not reflected in joined-up policy and service delivery. Tackling complex and deep-seated problems of urban regeneration and social exclusion demands far better collaboration between public bodies, and between them and the private and community sector, than we have become used to.

Holistic policy making and implementation of joined-up solutions will require a cultural revolution in four key respects. First of all, it demands an end to defensive, compartmentalised mentalities in the public sector at all levels, and a rejection of the competitive culture that fosters 'turf wars' between agencies and departments in central and local government. Second, it demands a reinvention of the relationship between central and local agencies, with far more trust, resources, power for innovation and responsibility for good outcomes being placed in the capacities of people at the grass roots where problems must be tackled and prevented. Third, it requires hard thinking about how we allocate resources to best effect – with a new focus on prevention and anticipation rather than reactive policies – and how we can measure *outcomes* holistically rather than becoming obsessed with inputs and outputs and a narrow, ultimately self-defeating idea of what counts as 'efficiency'. Finally, and most fundamentally, it requires a new bond of trust between public agencies and the citizen, building up trust and desire to participate in solving local problems after years of declining confidence among citizens in the public realm and their ability to help shape it.

These issues are central to the analysis presented here by David Wilkinson and Elaine Appelbee. Valuably, they focus on the many reforms and innovations we will need if we are to turn 'holistic government' and 'joined-up action' from high-minded aims and easy soundbites into real and lasting change in governance and in relations between public services and local communities. We at Demos hope that this timely study contributes to the development of a high-powered debate on how we make holistic government and holistic solutions to our 'wicked problems' a reality.

Ian Christie
Deputy Director, Demos

Editorial preface

For the first time in many years it is now possible to have an open and honest discussion about what John Stewart calls the 'wicked issues' in government. In health it is possible to acknowledge the vital importance of poverty, employment and social exclusion. The Green Paper, *Our healthier nation*, reminds us of all the factors that affect health.

Factors affecting health

Fixed	Social and economic	Environment	Lifestyle	Access to services
Genes	Poverty	Air quality	Diet	Education
Sex	Employment	Housing	Physical activity	NHS
Ageing	Social exclusion	Water quality	Smoking	Social services
		Social environment	Alcohol	Transport
			Sexual behaviour	Leisure
			Drugs	

If we are to improve health the NHS must work with everyone who can influence these factors – individuals, communities, voluntary groups, district and county councils, the Benefit Agency, schools and colleges, employers, the police and probation service, and those responsible for transport and economic development.

The NHS will not improve health by itself. David Wilkinson and Elaine Appelbee speak directly to all those concerned to tackle the 'wicked issues'. They challenge us to deliver joined up action on the ground. In order to do this we need "to change the culture of both service delivery and of citizen engagement with it." The greatest challenge is at local level. Powerful policies and frameworks are now in place – we have to find a way to make them real where it matters.

We must find the means to achieve "grounded change" and to do this we need to discover new ways to engage "those who are most affected by the consequences. People must be engaged in rebuilding their own quality of life in partnership with professionals, not in the latest manifestation of disempowered dependency."

It is not enough to make good use of 'special' funding at the margins of public resources. David and Elaine focus us back on the vast resources already available to the public services at local level: "sustainable improvement is dependent upon the integration and better application of mainstream spending." This powerful book challenges us to establish public enterprise, to discover "innovation and entrepreneurship ... which requires moral courage."

Leadership of the highest calibre is needed to achieve joined up action on the ground. David Wilkinson and Elaine Appelbee leave us in no doubt about what is required. To all those who aspire to leadership in local government, health, statutory and voluntary agencies and in the community itself, powerful advice is offered.

> **There is often a view that leaders need to be charismatic and perhaps aspire to hero status. This is mistaken. Effectiveness is more usually an outcome of determination, personal openness and the integrity and honesty experienced by others around them. Leaders communicate more by what they *do*, champion and support, than by what they *say*. They are able to substantially increase the stock of leadership across the system, generating a wide commitment to act, learn and take risks. It is the feedback from this that in turn sustains effective leaders. It is important that leaders find their own styles, and can act with a range of styles contingent upon the situation. Above all, they need to be able to live and work with paradox, dilemmas and uncertainty – both their own and others. *Courage* is probably more appropriate than *charisma*.**

This is a remarkable book – powerful, insightful and practical. If we follow the advice offered by David Wilkinson and Elaine Appelbee we will be closer to making a reality of joined-up action on the ground.

Ken Jarrold CBE
Chief Executive, County Durham Health Authority

Acknowledgements

There have been so many significant people who have helped shape our experience, knowledge, values and practice.

For many years we followed different career paths within the Bradford Metropolitan District, but unknown to each other – Elaine as a community development worker and David as a council officer. During this time Gordon Moore, to whom this book is dedicated, had a significant and hugely positive influence on both our careers. We met only recently through the suggestion of a third party, Val Mills, to whom we are particularly grateful. Since then we have worked jointly on the Centenary to Millennium Project (C2M) in Bradford and on the production of this report.

Our main purpose in putting this report together has been the desire to influence policy and practice. We believe that there is currently a window of opportunity. For too long, despite the promises of official rhetoric, real progress towards regeneration through local joined-up practice has been frustrated by actual policy implementation running counter to abundant available evidence. There is still a strong likelihood that the forces of the institutional status quo will continue for a while to absorb the impetus for radical reform. We believe firmly that the evidence of need for change will become invincible over the long term, even if progress is limited in the short term. Putting our case together has involved pulling together evidence and material from a wide range of different disciplines and spheres that normally remain in isolation, and also entering the worlds of influence previously unknown to us.

It may be unusual to write in these terms in a section on acknowledgements, but it has been an intensely personal and, at times, difficult experience. It is this context that has made the continuing support of two people so important to us. Ken Jarrold's swift and enthusiastic support for an early draft was of more significance than perhaps he will ever know. Similarly Ian Christie's unfailing encouragement and kindness for us to continue this project has been equally significant. Many others have been hugely influential. However, the responsibility for the text remains, of course, ours alone.

Our joint endeavours have been borne out of a need to act. Therefore we would like to recognise the work of a core group of people who made the birth of the C2M project possible: Geoff Reid, Ishtiaq Ahmed, Anthony Clipsom, Les Cousins, Mary Denholme, Bev Morton, Sandy Needham, Kathryn Paslawska, Ken Sutcliffe, and latterly, Pam Hardisty as well as the continuing support of Liam Hughes and David Kennedy, corporate directors at Bradford Metropolitan District Council. Similarly we would like to recognise the impact and influence of David Winchurch, Dick Hackett, Hardial Bhogul, Ken Thompson and John Davies in Walsall.

There are many others who have offered comment on previous drafts and ideas, either directly or through the Demos seminar process. In particular we would like to thank Judith Hunt, Nicky Gavron, Marilyn Taylor, Sue Richards, Peter Thompson, Perri 6, and Dick Atkinson.

We would also like to recognise both the support and constructive comments we have received from Ruth Badger, Robin Murray, Bob Garratt, Carol Hassan, Keith Barnes, Jim Brooks, Jo Whitehead, Roger Levitt, Helen Jones, Jane Winder, Dr Dorothy Birks and Liz McQue.

Finally, we would like to acknowledge the thoughtful and painstaking work of Dawn Louise Pudney, editorial manager at The Policy Press, and also that of Charles Leslie on a parallel document by the Local Government Management Board.

Elaine would like to thank all the people involved over the years in the Holmewood Parents Project and the Hutson Street Project whose ideas and actions have contributed significantly to some of the thinking in this report and to recognise especially the contribution of Tim Appelbee who, for more than 20 years, has willingly listened, supported and advised.

David would also like to appreciate the unfailing support he has received from his Whole System Development colleagues, Margaret Attwood and Mike Pedler. Thanks also to Katrina Wood for putting the manuscript together (many times!) and finally, and most significantly, to Maria Wilkinson for putting up with the endless disruptions that this 'cause' has led to.

Summary

The context (*Chapter 1*)

The new agenda for government in the twenty-first century is becoming clear. At its heart is the idea and the goal of ever more holistic government, built as much from the bottom up as from the top down. (6, 1997, p 70)

The shape of the Labour government's public and social policy intentions is now emerging. There is recognition that a series of intractable issues cannot be resolved in isolation. The causes of social exclusion, criminality, unemployment, poor health, low educational attainment, poor housing and welfare dependency are interlinked and multi-faceted. The Prime Minister has frequently talked of the need to keep the bigger picture in mind and called for "joined-up solutions for joined-up problems". After a year in government he has reiterated the point yet again. Writing in *The Observer*, he said:

Even the basic policies, targeted at unemployment, poor skills, low incomes, poor housing, high crime, bad health and family breakdown, will not deliver their full effect unless they are properly linked together. Joined-up problems need joined-up solutions. (*The Observer*, 31 May 1998)

The logic and need are compelling. However, the history of previous attempts to coordinate policy, together with both the growth of scale and the establishment of very different managerial and professional cultures across the agencies of delivery, do not suggest this will be easy.

But the requirement for delivering the new agenda – for modernisation – becomes ever more pressing because of another set of factors. Electorates are becoming increasingly socially liberal and fiscally conservative. And the pressures for international global competitiveness place further limits upon government's capacity to raise spending.

In particular this means that public institutions and agencies will need to favour strategies of provision geared more towards prevention rather than simply upon cure. For example, improvements in population health and longevity have always resulted far more from improvements in public health and social conditions than from investment in acute medical and surgical interventions. Similarly, long-term investment in *appropriate* crime prevention can reduce the reliance on highly expensive long-term custodial care with its high levels of recidivism.

However, this provides national government in particular with a dilemma. The new agenda of public reforms place great stress on public consultation and involvement, but, for the most part, there is, for example, strong public support for acute healthcare and heavy custodial sentencing. Hence, policy formulation and, in particular, implementation cannot follow a path of easy consumerism.

Government is going to have to involve and educate in the process of achieving demonstrable and perceptible outcomes. It needs to change the culture of both service delivery and of citizen engagement with it. It will have to run the risk of accusations of being a 'nanny' state, especially where it emphasises personal and collective obligations and responsibilities in balance with personal rights and choices.

This has highly significant implications at both the national, macro level as well as at the local micro level; in the myriad localities of implementation where joined-up *action* is a necessity. It is with this latter – effective local implementation – that this report is concerned. Policy intentions and frameworks are relatively clear. Hence, the concentration here is on the *how* of policy implementation rather than the *what*.

The implementation challenge (*Chapters 2 and 3*)

There is already a great deal known about how to achieve integrated working on the ground that focuses upon outcomes directed towards the improvement of the quality of life for citizens. While this is increasingly starting to inform aspects of national policy, sadly it remains either unknown or little understood across most public service delivery agencies.

For the most part, current government reforms and proposals provide welcome frameworks for implementation of this empirically derived knowledge (see Box 1) – change that works. But they will require two major *linked* shifts in the cultures of public service delivery.

Box 1: Current government reform

- Setting up of the Social Exclusion Unit.
- The report by the Social Exclusion Unit, *Bringing Britain together: A national strategy for neighbourhood renewal*, establishing the new pathfinder regeneration scheme.
- Establishment of action zones for health, education and employment.
- Targeting of the 'worst estates' in Britain.
- Reform of local government being the price for greater autonomy; the Best Value initiative, the establishment of beacon councils, and new forms of executive governance.
- The establishment of new partnerships under the Crime and Disorder Bill.
- Plans for strengthening community leadership and government through community level planning.
- Obligation upon local government to act collaboratively and to promote the economic, social and environmental well-being of their area.
- Increasing the emphasis on capacity building and developing social cohesion, especially in its regeneration initiatives.
- Removing the emphasis on short-term internal competitive markets and contracts and moving towards longer-term models of collaboration and contestability.
- The new emphasis in health on collaborative working, health improvement programmes, formation of primary care groups and the development of healthy living centres.
- Less dependency and strengthening self-sufficiency.
- Increasing stress on sustainable economic, environmental and social improvement; the quality of life agenda.
- The plethora of consultation papers, green and white papers relating to health and local government.

Firstly, they will have to overcome their predisposition to attempt top-down implementation within the confines of narrow departmentally, professionally and managerially driven solutions. This will require that they move towards real partnership and innovations based upon learning from both good practice outside and through their own successes and failures of implementation. Paper plans are not implementation. There are no simple blueprints. They have to get beyond the endless rhetoric of partnership, learning organisations, empowerment and so on, to real grounded change; beyond the ever more sophisticated language and paper plans on the input side, to achievable holistic outcomes. To be sure, such back-of-house, process changes are critical as means to ends. But the focus must be tied to outcomes that lie outside the formal boundaries of professional organisation.

Secondly, in order to achieve this, public services will need to develop new ways of reconnecting with their publics. The historic growth in professional, managerial, political and union hierarchy and resulting power balances has frequently led to producer capture at the expense of user engagement. More recent reforms such as compulsory competitive tendering (CCT), devolved agencies, and so-called internal markets put a welcome emphasis on efficiencies and to some extent on short-term outputs, but has often increased defensive, non-collaborative 'silo-based' behaviour. The result has been increasing fragmentation of provision, low levels of trust, and disconnection from an increasingly dependent public. The requirement is for people and communities to take more proactive roles in understanding their own needs and for sustaining civic society. This requires much more than well-intentioned consultation exercises that feed the paper output of semi-detached policy planners. In particular, if we are to tackle the wicked issues of crime, poverty, poor health, and low educational attainment, that have been the main public concerns for the last 40 years, then we must engage all the resources at our disposal. This has to include those who are most affected by the consequences. People must be engaged in rebuilding their own quality of life in partnership with professionals, not in the latest manifestation of disempowered dependency.

There is a good deal of enthusiasm for the new change agenda across the public services. But this future energy will need to be focused, persistent and driven from a clear vision of the bigger future of change that works.

There has also been a burgeoning of partnerships between local delivery agencies and wider groups of stakeholders. Many of these were formed in response to a variety of regeneration initiatives. But they are also developing in profusion in response to the new public service agenda. In the main, they are ad hoc and arise in relation to specific, usually district-wide needs that relate to specific initiatives such as developing primary care groups, health improvement initiatives, the Crime and Disorder Bill, regeneration projects, LA21 initiatives and so on. In addition to these are the growing requirements to consult and involve the public. The danger is that this plethora of partnering and consulting will generate large amounts of input activity for headquarters staff and an increasingly bemused and angry population experiencing consultation fatigue especially in more deprived localities. Similarly, front-line staff who are held to account to meet departmentally-based criteria, will see calls for closer working to be little more than extra tasks to feed the requirements of the corporate centre.

This constitutes a *third* challenge: how to engage service users, citizens and front-line staff across agencies in ways that address the new agendas that are *meaningful to them?* Further, how can such apparent top-down complexity yield to a coherent bottom-up simplicity that is owned, designed and delivered by newly energised front-line staff and citizens? How is the wealth of essential knowledge that they hold going to be brought in so that sustainable change can be achieved?

Change that works (*Chapters 4, 5 and 6*)

Fortunately a good deal is known about change that works – change that does make a sustainable difference to the quality of life, especially in Britain's poorer communities. This can be looked at from three linked perspectives:

- multi-agency front-line working and sustainable community development;
- the critical path to organisational/agency renewal;
- the growth of social and civic entrepreneurs, self-help and voluntary activity.

Multi-agency front-line working and sustainable improvements to the quality of life (Chapter 4)

Multi-agency front-line working is the key to making a lasting difference. It is the critical arena where top-down can reconnect with bottom-up; where different professionals, each with their own differently derived professional models for diagnoses and service remedies, can begin to engage with each other and community members. Professional knowledge, in the past so often separated from context, becomes informed by knowledge of local needs and contexts. Reconnection can start by front-line professionals (used generically here to include all front-line workers and their immediate managers) and local people engaging in a longer-term discussion about problems and potential solutions. This might start with a few people, but will seek to include wider circles of people over time.

These early discussions can often be contentious and filled with anger and unrealistic expectations. But with persistence this can change very quickly and many are concerned that public money is better spent. There is sadness when improvements to the physical infrastructure – housing renovations, landscaping, play areas etc – have been trashed and vandalised. There is a realisation that improvements to the social infrastructure must proceed alongside improvements to the physical.

From this growing dialogue, collective pictures of future improvements can be built. What could this neighbourhood be like in five years? What changes/improvements do we need to make to work towards this? What must we avoid doing?

A series of significant, linked streams of activity can start to flow from this. Typically it becomes possible to develop clarity about holistic outcomes that are widely shared and understood. These cannot be achieved without all making contributions, professionals and community. And each needs the others to reach their own goals. Empty houses cannot be filled and looked after, without improvements to the neighbourhood as a whole and community safety in particular. Health improvements may only follow raising people's perception of self-worth through addressing their issues of child and community safety, isolation, exclusion and unemployment. Reduction of long-term criminality will depend upon targeted policing, but in collaboration with longer-term educational processes, improved parenting, youth facilities and target hardening (making theft and vandalism more difficult). Schools can make a difference to educational attainment in isolation. But how much better if there is greater parental involvement, particularly in pre and early school years.

Likewise many critical aspects of well-being and quality of life can only be improved by people themselves coming together to assess needs, provide forums for activity and community facilities. It is through this that social networks of trust and greater cohesiveness can be rebuilt and people's sense of self-worth improved.

Both mainstream service delivery and any specific regeneration monies needs to support the rebuilding of social cohesion and social know-how (capacity building). Too often in the past this simply has not happened. Worse, the ties that already existed have been either ignored or even weakened, by the intervention of well meaning, but unintentionally, arrogant professional, managerial and political leadership.

The empirical evidence for the success of local partnerships between empowered multi-agency front-line staff and local neighbourhoods is extremely strong. This then must be the central focus for tackling the wider issues and social improvement; it is the key to joined-up action.

And the partnerships – both between professionals themselves, and between professional groups and neighbourhoods – are not about consultations and occasional meeting. They require involvement by all the local stakeholders, interdependence and each seeing their contributions to a shared bigger picture of improvement and action.

Critically, the *vertical* networks of power, resources and professional activity, have to be translated into *horizontal* networks of durability, trust and loyalty. Of course there will be dispute, tension and unfulfilled expectation. This is probably both inevitable and an important part of the trust-building process. It favours voice and contestability, rather than exit and short-term distrustful contracting. This both feeds, and is supported by, the growth of empowered front-line multi-agency teams working with community stakeholders, monitoring and reviewing their own progress and adjusting their plans accordingly.

In this context the role of district-wide partnerships becomes strategic and direction giving. It needs to clarify the frameworks for partnerships as well as for processes of consultation and involvement. District-wide partners should provide overall coherence and simplicity and chart how the process should work. They need to create the conditions for empowered multi-agency front-line teams, and the systems and the organisational infrastructure for their support, while holding them accountable for outcomes. The engagement with communities and provision of holistic budgets will place a discipline on the achievement of holistic outcomes geared to improving the quality of life.

There will be non-formulaic, one-size-fits-all, approach for doing this. Each locality will be different with different resources and existing conditions. Significant innovations may already exist that need to be built upon. These could be housing, police, health or education led for example. Similarly the 'starting strength' could be with a community-based initiative, such as a community trust or other act of social entrepreneuralism.

Some district-wide partners may wish to cover different localities in different ways. They may set up front-line teams in a limited number of localities, choosing to work with other areas of concern and/or social groupings over a bigger or 'whole district' area. Clearly, experimentation, innovation and learning are required. Because of the public service 'silo' inheritance this will be difficult and demanding. But the key to joined-up action lies with empowered front-line multi-agency teams accountable for holistic outcomes linked to improving the quality of life. And without community engagement and involvement this simply cannot be done.

Finally it must be emphasised that the key to sustainable improvements is dependent upon the integration and better application of mainstream spending. Of course, extra funding through regeneration projects does bring benefit, but only if it is fully linked into the delivery of mainstream services and marries improvements to both hard and soft neighbourhood infrastructures. All too frequently, despite the lip service, this has not happened.

Sustaining organisational and whole system change (Chapter 5)

Policy makers and those with a strategic role in local implementation should be under no illusions about how profound these changes may be and how long they will take.

Quasi-Fordist and Taylorist approaches to organisation and management have long dominated public services. These emphasise the separation of planning from action; of thinking from doing. Its guiding metaphor is that of the organisation as machine largely assuming linear connections between cause and effect, the division of the whole into parts with carefully planned description of jobs together with the vertical and horizontal division of labour. Hierarchies of vertical control, supervision and specialised inspection functions supposedly ensure quality.

Work procedures are specified by 'external' expertise in organisation and methods, and work study. They assume low trust, whatever the formal rhetoric. In effect, workers are encouraged to follow the formal rules and 'leave their brains at the door'.

Post-Taylorist models turn this upside down, emphasising flexibility, multi-skilling, team work, often self-managing, vertical and horizontal job integration, reconnecting thinking and doing, and involving everybody in monitoring, and self and team inspection, as the basis for continual improvement. They follow cross-boundary working across organisations and along buyer–supplier chains with processes of parallel design, and networking. The emphasis is on the development of high trust cultures through long-term contracts, voice and loyalty rather than distrust promoted by short-term defensive contracting, externalising costs onto others and exit.

The post-Taylorist model was developed in the first place in a few locations in the Japanese car industry from an amalgam of American, British and Japanese ideas and practices. Despite the Anglo-American sources, Western manufacturing has found considerable difficulty altering its mental models, behaviour and practices. At root, this is why we have in Britain the most productive car plant in Europe, perhaps the world, in Japanese ownership and no indigenous car industry of our own.

There is a further difficulty. Many of these post–Taylorist ideas and processes have been attempted by Western and British management including public services. For example, approaches to quality frequently become packaged into training programmes and procedural manuals. In effect, they are 'programmed' back into Taylorist methods to sell to the predominating, reductionist mind–set of the Anglo–American manager – public and private. This leads to widespread bewilderment and confusion, especially for middle managers and front–line staff. Top management language is redolent with post–Taylorist words and ideas, but action and behaviour are rooted in the old mind–sets, assumptions and guiding metaphors. Thus it seems, whatever the problem, the answer is restructuring, more training and more control.

This is why so many attempts to implement radical change, new ways of working and changed working cultures are so often disappointing. There is widespread agreement in the research literature that 75% of change efforts fail. And it should be transparently clear that such top-down, programmatic, formulaic approaches to change management driven from the machine metaphor cannot deliver the new change agenda, especially the improvement of front–line multi–agency service delivery, so vital in tackling issues of social deprivation and fragmentation. The styles of management involved would simply kill empowered front-line multi–agency team working. Management rhetoric would support it; the reality will be very different.

Again, it is quite possible to develop appropriate post–Taylorist approaches to change management from a range of empirical studies of successful change in both public and private sectors. In essence, they embrace the assumptions set out above; they work with whole system and action learning perspective, and place particular emphasis on new forms of leadership and inclusivity.

Critically, leaders have to translate external pressures into dissatisfaction with the status quo and excitement about a better way. Dissatisfaction is fuelled by confronting people with the realisation that current approaches are no longer effective in meeting the new demands. Excitement is stimulated by encouraging people, especially those at, and near to, front–line delivery, to explore new ways that address current problems and appeal to fundamental values.

Effective change leaders also demonstrate a range of significant *behaviours* which give credibility to what they say.

In leading and promoting whole system changes, effective leaders typically follow a critical path. Firstly, they create a readiness for change through an appropriate mix of disturbance, challenge and support.

Secondly, they work towards the informal redefinition of roles, responsibilities and relationships around the key tasks and priorities that have to be achieved. This necessitates that those involved have to develop new ways of working and learning together in order to understand and solve new questions and challenges.

Thirdly, they support and encourage team members to learn new skills and knowledge that they find they need in order to develop the new competencies required. This is likely to include skills of working together and with the wider system, in pursuit of the emerging new objectives. It is through these second and third 'stages' that attitudes and working cultures start to change as a response to the need to do things differently. The key is the creation of receptive conditions for change, not top-down attempts to prescribe attitude and culture changes. Fourthly, they promote the bottom-up improvement of systems to support the new flexible teamwork focused upon task achievement. These systems can include appraisal, training needs analysis, career development, management direction and support and so on.

Fifthly, they modify organisation structures and information, monitoring, and compensation systems to consolidate the new configurations of working. Structure follows function. They recognise that attitude and culture changes follow the newly required behaviours and competencies.

It is through such processes that effective leaders produce extraordinary results. They are notable because they are able to escape from the swamps of Taylorist thinking and habituated approaches to change management.

The growth of social and civic entrepreneurs, self-help and voluntary activity (Chapter 6)

It is widely presumed that the traditional bonds of social cohesion are weakening, particularly those associated with communities of place. This is perhaps most marked in some of the more deprived areas. However, it is possible to point to the emergence of significant countervailing trends over the last decade.

For instance, Charles Leadbeater has identified the risk of social and civic entrepreneurs who seek to bring together resources, often previously underutilised, to create social capital, relationships, networks of trust and cooperation that can give access to financial and physical assets. Their goals are social, not primarily for profit. The beneficiaries are members rather than shareholders. They are social entrepreneurs because they are part of civic society rather than state; frequently they may be at odds with official bodies in the public domain.

They are innovative in seeing new ways to tackle issues of regeneration and the promotion of health, welfare and well-being. While they frequently create physical resources, these are always the means rather than the end itself. It is the social outcomes and the building of social capital that mark achievement. They seek to develop the most underused asset of all, the previously excluded.

There are now a variety of schemes designed to give support to emerging social entrepreneurs. These are designed to put them in contact with one another, to promote the transfer of ideas and learning, and to cut down the sense of isolation that can occur, especially where both immediate resources and official/agency support are low.

There has been a burgeoning of similar social and largely voluntary innovative activity. These, for example, include the rise of development trusts, LETS schemes, credit unions, environmental and recycling groups, LA21 initiatives, volunteer schemes, and community capacity building projects. The scale of these activities should not be underestimated, especially considering the low level of official support such activities have often received.

Charles Leadbeater has recently extended his ideas of entrepreneurship to include some who work within the state sector in parallel ways. Their achievement is to be similarly creative in terms of pooling and building resources to yield improved social outcomes.

While they may have more resources at their disposal (and perhaps a wider range of contacts with the agencies – at least theoretically), they have to operate within the particular constrains of often narrow political and managerial accountability. This poses the dilemma of 'being innovative while staying within the rules'. Taylorist systems do not usually appreciate innovation near the front line, whatever the declared rhetoric. Huge efforts may be put into minimising and dismissing achievement because it represents a disruption to the 'smooth running' of the machine. Of course, it also serves to show up its failings which are usually carefully hidden. Tellingly, Leadbeater produces the following working definition:

Civic entrepreneurship is the renegotiation of the mandate and sense of a public organisation, which allows it to find new ways of combining resources and people, both public and private, to deliver social outcomes, higher social values

and more social capital. (Leadbeater and Goss, 1998, pp 16–17)

For example, he illustrates one aspect of this in his case study of Norma Redfearn and her staff at a primary school in a highly deprived area of Newcastle. In order to turn round a near failing school she decided that she had to work with the development and involvement of the whole community – the school becoming a community resource and linking into other services. She and her staff concentrated on the bigger picture, paying less immediate attention to the official short-term goals of improving numbers, attendance and test results. Over the longer period, these showed huge improvements, but only as a result of success in achieving the wider social outcomes.

In all too many of our public service bodies, innovation and entrepreneurship are activities which require moral courage and may well incur the wrath of higher authority. By definition, any act of innovation will stimulate disturbance, tension and resistance. They cannot be done by numbers. But many of our institutions will have to become more nurturing of innovation.

Attempts to develop more civic entrepreneurs as the main strategy for public service change are likely to be frustrated by predominantly Taylorist cultures and organisational infrastructure. Frequently this will lead to organisations speaking with opposite voices – 'please be entrepreneurial but do it by the book'. Of course this will never be said, but that is how it will be widely read, except by the most determined and single-minded. At least as much attention will need to be given to the development of receptive conditions for civic entrepreneurship and the growth of organisational-wide learning.

Finally, it is important to recognise especially the rise of self-help groups, especially around health and caring issues, as part of a rapidly changing and growing voluntary sector. These have often campaigned and negotiated for better, more appropriate care and support for long-term sufferers and their carers. They have also had significant results in clinical and professional practice, the treatment of Aids and breast cancer being two particular examples. In so many arenas, professional practice can only improve by working in close and involved partnership 'with those living the journey'.

The content of this report has both influenced and been influenced by the developing *C2M project* in the Bradford Metropolitan District. This project seeks to:

- strengthen the capacity of local communities, especially their ability to audit and take action in support of their own needs – building local agendas;
- improve the links between, and learning across, the many diverse communities that make up the district;
- enable public institutions and agencies especially to become better partners each with the express purpose of becoming effective partners with local communities.

(The C2M case study is presented on pp 112-18.)

Policies which aim to promote partnership and joined-up policies to produce both more effective services and tackle the more intractable social problems, must encourage rather than inhibit social and civic entrepreneurship and innovation. All too frequently such activity is ignored or even opposed. This is all the more disappointing when regeneration projects work in this way; where they are driven by unreconstituted narrow officer agendas, reflecting the limited goals and interests of individual service silos, and where the emphasis is upon the achievement of short-term hard physical outputs. All the evidence suggests that such projects may well yield short-term results in hard infrastructure; those aspects which can be easily counted. But usually this will not be sustainable; the long-term costs and waste will be enormous. That, of course, is what the American statistician and quality guru, W. Edward Deming, taught Japanese manufacturers during the 1950s and 1960s. It is not a lesson that British management, public or private, finds easy to absorb. Prevention always produces both better quality and long-term efficiencies than cure. But that means moving from an over-reliance on vertical top-down, end-of-the-line inspection towards horizontal team-based, self-inspection and continual improvement linked to the attainment of holistic outcomes.

Improving sustainable quality of life: the benchmark for Best Value (*Chapter 7*)

The last three sections have focused on what works from three differing, but related, perspectives. They have focused primarily on social and economic well-being.

However, alongside this have to be matched the increasing public concerns about environmental deterioration from local to global perspectives.

A number of local authorities in particular have pioneered innovative local and neighbourhood level programmes to engage public interest through the adoption of Local Agenda 21 (LA21). The government, in collaboration with the Local Government Association (LGA) and the Local Government Management Board (LGMB), have recently launched new guidelines on LA21. Sir Jeremy Beecham, as Chair of the LGA, has written to all local authority leaders and chief executives that, "The new frameworks and processes that will flow from the *joint central and local government agenda to revitalise local government – for example on Best Value, local community leadership, and democratic renewal –* will in turn provide opportunities to support and deliver the objectives of Local Agenda 21."

It is encouraging that some important links are being made here. Increasingly economic, social and environmental improvements are seen as irrevocably interconnected, especially when viewed with the long view in mind. Thus, sustainability has to be achieved through improvement to quality of life as a whole. Further, the thrust of LA21 activity, and emerging good practice, stresses the requirement to link public involvement and participation at the local/neighbourhood level to wider populations and geographies – from local to global. The frame of action parallels the one that emerges for change that works in the social, economic and organisational spheres. From holistic systems perspectives this is, of course, hardly surprising.

But because of the functionalist Fordist and Taylorist traditions of public sector institutions and agencies, this is not easy to achieve. In particular, it raises four sets of related issues.

Firstly, we have inherited the disconnection of land-use planning from other forms of planning – economic, housing, transport, financial, environmental, education and so on. There is a need therefore to rethink and reconnect the horizontal and vertical integration of planning systems.

Secondly, we have learned (or have we?) that this cannot be done by grand top-down designs. Involvement and participation at the local level is of paramount importance. The integration of planning systems is more about frameworks and processes than content and control. New ways of linking top-down and bottom-up are required.

Thirdly, there is a need to be far clearer about the differences, connections, roles and purposes of public involvement, participation and consultation. Currently it seems that the terms are used interchangeably in the mass of directives and advice coming through the silos of government departments. This is of particular significance in so many regeneration projects, where official bodies talk of participation and empowerment when the experienced reality is the flimsiest of consultation done, more to satisfy the top-down predilections of the Government Regional Office than with any real intention to reconnect with the public in a different way.

Fourthly, the operation of Best Value in local government is going to be crucial; it has the capacity to make or break holistic implementation. If it works for improvement of service quality on a service-by-service basis, its impact will be to reinforce the functional inheritance. On the other hand, it could be the vital ingredient in the pursuit of horizontal and vertical integration, the linking of top-down and bottom-up and connecting the neighbourhood to district and region.

Six key issues that have to be addressed (*Chapter 8*)

The report highlights six key issues that will have to be addressed if the necessary innovations are to occur on the ground. These six issues constitute a fundamental challenge to the current workings and cultures of public services, and especially to those services in local government whose lead role will be so vital in the changes that are required.

1. **Developing evidence-based approaches to change – using the research:** Perhaps the saddest and most frustrating aspect of so much change effort is the widespread ignorance of what works – this is all the more poignant where social and economic regeneration initiatives are concerned. In part, this may be because much of the evidence, not surprisingly, points to multi-pronged, multi-agency interventions into complex systems of causation. Therefore, it can be easily read – if read at all – as falling into other people's domains. Much of it can be seen as 'something to do with community development' and therefore separate from the components of service delivery. It will be difficult to move forward until a critical mass of service deliverers recognise the impact of their services, both historically and currently, on communities.

2. **Recovery from addiction to failing ways of working:** The single biggest danger with the new wave of public service reforms is that those with executive authority for implementation will trigger an unprecedented number of top-down initiatives and projects. These will become ever more time-consuming and complex because of the emphasis on partnership working which will be translated as a series of top-down managing and planning mechanisms. Means

will become ends. Process improvement will be detached from outcomes and the focus will go internal. The predominating interest will once again be on inputs and top-down indicators of success. In no time we will have an array of indications that purport to measure the effectiveness of partnerships but that are themselves quite disconnected from the real need for partnership on the ground.

3. **Taking community involvement seriously:** The arguments for this are largely prosaic and rooted in notions of longer-term enlightened self-interest of those concerned. The reasons why community involvement and capacity building are essential in so many neighbourhoods are:
   - All the evidence says so.
   - Local people know most about local conditions. They can be crucial in both the diagnosis of the systemic causes of problems and who should be engaged in their amelioration. They also know about existing community networks and how to develop these rather than having them ruptured by clumsy top-down interventions. In regeneration projects especially, entry strategies are at least as important as exit strategies.
   - It is through the development of local agendas and the active participation of community partnerships that accountability for holistic outcomes can be maintained. Without this, internal silo agendas may usurp them.
   - Social capital can only be rebuilt by people themselves taking responsibility for its creation. It is the role of front-line professions to deliver services in concert to assist this.
   - It is the central means whereby critical masses of local people own the small improvements that start to make the difference and have a huge stake in their sustainability.
   - It acts as the continuing and developing outward focus to meld the best of the various professional knowledges with knowledge of local circumstances and conditions. Professional practice is improved as a result of working closely with those living the journey.
   - Well-developed community partnerships and membership arrangements (including the possibility of local representative democracy) provide for continuity of external outcome focus and lessen the possibility of capture and entryism by unrepresentative voices.

- It is an important stepping stone for many to start connecting beyond the confines and isolation of the local patch.
- It is the most effective way to start connecting with any existing social and civic entrepreneurs, self-help groups and so on, as well as providing fertile ground for promoting the development of these activities.

4. **Getting beyond zero-sum power games and establishing trust:** While there is much more recognition of the need to achieve win-win outcomes where there is conflict and/or division, much top management behaviour appears to derive from a deeper assumption that there is only a limited amount of power available to drive and control the organisation (or machine). This corresponds to a similar conception of the limits of available resources. When so much professional activity appears based on deficit models of client and community needs – on what people have not 'got' – this accentuates both lack of power and resources to change. Driven from these perspectives, management becomes more a matter of control, doing what can be done and keeping the lid on any number of impending crises – keeping the machine on track. Such organisations are forever held on the curative path.

5. **Best Value: the making or breaking of holistic government:** Simply defined, Best Value places an obligation on a local authority to continually search to improve the quality, effectiveness and efficiency of all its activities and service delivery to the public. Local authorities are usually going to be a vital component of locally-based strategies to tackle social exclusion, regeneration and sustainable curative government despite the range of other agencies that are essential to success. Thus, the way in which local authorities approach Best Value is an issue of the utmost importance.

6. **Real change takes time:** Invariably, in any given location and context, it has taken many years for current states to be as they are; they are the outcome of complex system dynamics that involve people in communities and a myriad of agencies, institutions and external influences. In all likelihood it will take many years to produce the greatly superior outcomes that can be produced by shifting to greater preventative, quality of life, culture changing focus.

Working in the middle ground: recommendations to promote joined-up action on the ground (*Chapter 9*)

The key role of executive implementor is to create, through genuine engagement between themselves, strategic back-line partnership to create the conditions and mechanisms for effective neighbourhood-level front-line partnership working. The recommendations are designed to promote this and work against the endemic preoccupation with these central and corporate issues that can become dangerously disconnected from the intentions of the reforms. Their purpose is to put attention and resourcing into the gap and spaces that are largely ignored:

- between people in local communities;
- between communities and neighbourhoods themselves;
- between the agencies enabling them to become better partners with citizens and local communities;
- between the agencies' and citizens'/communities.

This new focus on the 'middle ground' – the gap between 'bottom up' and 'top down' and the horizontal divisions between communities and between agencies – is designed to ensure that the progressive transformation of the public services is formed on holistic outcomes for citizens and communities, *as expressed by them*. There is a high requirement for this reconnection. Sadly, the resources of time and money are locked up *within* current institutional cultural and control systems. New seed resources, together with incentives and penalties, need to change this by rewarding collaborative activity and *learning through action* to overcome this endemic tendency.

The recommendations then cover eight linked areas of policy and its implementation.

1. **Developing 'middle ground' activity.** Government, through the newly emerging Regional Development Agencies (RDAs), should actively promote innovative and facilitative projects such as C2M in Bradford. Their roles would cover some or all of the following:
   - stimulating community and neighbourhood-based audit, planning and action;
   - connecting existing and emerging community activists, energisers and social entrepreneurs with each other and across counties and districts;
   - enabling agencies to become better partners with communities (and by implication with each other).

2. **Adjusting regeneration funding regimes** to provide a larger number of very much smaller grants to actively promote neighbourhood capacity building. Bids for larger sums of money should be community-led as an outcome of previous capacity building. Development of social infrastructure should precede and support improvements to physical infrastructure.

3. **Developing empowered multi-agency front-line teams.** Getting better value from mainstream spending lies at the core of modernising public services. It is clear that the way to do this is through their reconfiguration around neighbourhood agendas. This should not be seen as just a component of regeneration projects. It should be applied much more widely to include areas that do not fit official definitions of deprivation. There should be increasing use of pooled front-line multi-agency budgets, with teams held accountable for achieving holistic outcomes that link directly to the improvement of quality of life as experienced by residents.

4. **Action research and development and learning** should be sponsored through a newly-formed Public Service Development Board.

5. **Social housing policy** should increasingly encourage tenant ownership, participation and the building of social communities.

6. **Planning systems** require greater vertical and horizontal simplification, coordination and integration.

7. There needs to be protection, and the progressive increase of, activities, budgets, professional development and career pathways that favour prevention through the tackling of systemic causation.

8. **Beacon status** should only be awarded to those public bodies that can demonstrate their active reconnection to local communities through genuine multi-agency partnership leading to the attainment of holistic outcomes.

ONE

Setting the context

The new agenda for government in the twenty-first century is becoming clear. At its heart is the idea and the goal of ever more holistic government, built as much from the bottom up as from the top down. (6, 1997, p 70)

The shape of the new Labour government's public and social policy intentions is now emerging. There is recognition that a series of intractable issues cannot be resolved in isolation. The causes of social exclusion, criminality, unemployment, poor health, low educational attainment, poor housing and welfare dependency, are interlinked and multi-faceted. The Prime Minister has frequently talked of the need to keep the bigger picture in mind and called for "joined-up solutions for joined-up problems" (*The Times*, 9 December 1997: leader column referring to the Prime Minister's launch of the Social Exclusion Unit the day before). After a year in government he has reiterated the point yet again. Writing in *The Observer* he says,

Even the basic policies, targeted at unemployment, poor skills, low incomes, poor housing, high crime, bad health and family breakdown, will not deliver their full effect unless they are properly linked together. Joined-up problems need joined-up solutions. (*The Observer*, 31 May 1998)

The logic and need are compelling. However, the history of previous attempts to coordinate policy, together with both the growth of scale and the establishment of very different managerial and professional cultures across the agencies of delivery, do not suggest this will be easy. It will require a major shift towards lateral working across different agencies in partnership with local neighbourhoods. While the new rhetoric is being advanced in every quarter, it is likely that the reality of implementation will be strongly resisted. There are two central reasons for this. Firstly, a great many people have an enormous investment in the power bases, career structures and the management, political and professional cultures of the status quo. These are essentially hierarchical and asymmetrical in relation to the horizontal and self-generating linkages required for change. Secondly, this status quo is reinforced by the historical emphasis on cure of the presenting problems rather than prevention in the first place. It is a Fordist rather than a quality approach. Making the switch towards longer-term prevention is likely to prove very difficult in many areas of provision.

At the same time, political analysts have described the development of a new political culture in post-industrial societies (see Clark, 1997 and Rempel and Clark, 1997). These highlight the electoral significance of an increasing middle class broadly described as socially liberal and fiscally conservative. This suggests the development of fiscal populism which downplays ideology, "opposes patronage, supports clean government and makes extensive use of electoral media in campaigns" (Clark and Rempel, 1997, p 5). The government is developing its own responses to this in its tight adherence to public spending targets and the exploration of a third way[1]. In a highly significant article (for the analysis and recommendations in this report), Peter Kellner proposes the idea of mutualism – "the doctrine that individual and collective well-being is attainable only by mutual dependence" (Kellner, 1998, pp 30-2).

Perri 6 sums up the dilemma thus:

> **Governments remain saddled with a problem they cannot solve. After a century of growth, governments in all western countries are now caught between the public's resistance to paying tax and their rising demand for the provision of welfare, education, healthcare, infrastructure and social order. (6, 1997, p 13)**

Therefore, the attention needs to move towards addressing causes of social problems and enabling people themselves to develop the confidence, skills and social infrastructure to do this. This suggests a very different relationship between the public and the services provided through public funding.

This report assumes 'the watchwords for the next generation of government reformers', as set out by Perri 6, namely,

- holistic government
- preventative government
- culture-changing government
- outcome-oriented government.

It also accepts and welcomes many of the possibilities inherent in the government's policy developments and outline proposals:

- Setting up of the Social Exclusion Unit.
- The report by the Social Exclusion Unit, *Bringing Britain together: A national strategy for neighbourhood renewal*, establishing the new pathfinder regeneration scheme.
- Establishment of action zones in health, education and employment.
- Targeting of the 20 'worst estates' in Britain.
- Reform of local government being the price for greater autonomy; and the Best Value initiative.
- Plans for strengthening community leadership and government through community-level planning.
- Obligation upon local government to act collaboratively and to promote the economic, social and environmental well-being of their area.
- Increasing the emphasis on capacity building and developing social cohesion, especially in its regeneration initiatives.
- Removing the emphasis on short-term internal competitive markets and contracts and moving towards longer-term models of collaboration and contestability.
- Less dependency and strengthening self-sufficiency.
- The plethora of consultation papers, green and white papers, relating to health and local government.

It is difficult to doubt the seriousness of the commitment to change. However, there are some fundamental difficulties in implementing this ambitious agenda that will require tough, radical and practical action at the local level, otherwise the rhetoric–reality gap will grow ever wider. Joined-up policy clearly requires joined-up action on the ground. The historical precedents for this are not promising to put it mildly. Turf wars have always been endemic to the public services – and outside – whether at the levels of government, civil service or delivery on the ground. This has increased in direct relation to their postwar growth, often exacerbated by a limiting view of playing at markets. Further, at the local level, the gap between these services and 'their public' has been growing. This is especially so in local government where public and community endeavour is largely disconnected from the political, professional and managerial hierarchies. This was symbolised by the historically low turnout figures for the May 1998 local elections.

At government levels it is already suggested that some ministers, and/ or their departments, are more adept than others at keeping the big picture in mind; at working holistically. What chance, then, local government, health and the police in hundreds of different districts, contexts and even more localities across the UK? Top-down fiat will not achieve what historically (and perhaps currently?) government finds so hard itself.

Box 2: The Joint Approach to Social Policy – Lessons from the past?

W. Plowden ('Unit costs, *The Guardian*, 7 January 1998) describes the failure 20 years ago of the Joint Approach to Social Policy (JASP) led by the Rothschild (and later Berrill) 'think-tank', the Central Policy Review Staff (CPRS). In an extremely pertinent article, Plowden makes two particularly telling points. Firstly, 'the official machine' has probably forgotten all about JASP and what could be learned from that experience. The inability of public services to learn caused, in part at least, by corporate amnesia and myopia, is a continuing theme in this report. Secondly, "Whitehall can, and often does preach co-ordination, but it cannot do it. That has to be left to people on the ground. Only they can put together, and manage, effective 'packages' of service."

The initial responses to the new change agenda by much of local government appear to typify the problem. The government has put forward a range of innovations and appears to be asking local authorities to provide a range of innovative, integrated responses to these proposals based on its local knowledge, context and conditions, and to do this through extensive partnerships with other agencies. On the other hand, the typical response seems to be, tell us exactly what you want for each project and we will do it, and can we have our old financial autonomy back as well, please? Much of local government appears trapped in a resentful, dependency relationship with the centre in much the same way as it holds its more impoverished citizens and communities. Thus the flow of innovative, proactive responses by individual authorities is low, and from the local government community as a whole, even lower (see Travers and Jones, 1998, p 16, who say that "local government finds it impossible to publish and debate even mildly radical ideas"). *The new commitment to regeneration* from the Local Government Association could be a promising exception to this (Pathfinders, Circular 226/98, LGA, 2 April 1998: LGA, 26 Chapter Street, London SW1P 4ND).

This report makes a number of proposals to address these issues.

They are concerned with the *how* of policy implementation, rather than the *what*. The rhetoric–reality gap in policy making and implementation is a recurrent theme. They are rooted in the lessons that can be learned from empirically-based studies of change that works. They are also designed to help integrate and simplify the potential for radically transforming and improving the delivery of public services inherent in the programme of government reforms. However, without very different approaches to leading organisational and inter-agency change, this potential will remain largely unfulfilled. Already, it is becoming apparent that many public bodies are becoming overwhelmed by the sheer volume of change initiatives coming top-down, made worse because they are so often seen as disconnected change projects. Nor should the enormous resistance to change resulting from the inherited institutional legacy be underestimated. This is given full focus in Chapter 8 – six key issues that have to be addressed. The proposals themselves are described in Chapter 9.

Note

[1] The subject of media speculation, highlighted by reports on what may have taken place at a seminar with the Prime Minister at No 10 Downing Street on Thursday 7 May 1998. See especially reports in *The Observer* and the *Sunday Times* on 10 May 1998 for somewhat different accounts of this. For the clearest current articulation of the 'third way' so far, see Giddens, 1998.

TWO

The functional inheritance and its consequences

... established social systems absorb agents of change and de-fuse, dilute and turn to their own ends the energies originally directed towards change.... When processes embodying threat cannot be repelled, ignored, contained or transformed, social systems tend to respond by change – but the *least change* capable of neutralising or meeting the intrusive process. (Schon, 1971, p 40)

The functional model has been the dominant organising principle throughout the growth of the welfare state. Perri 6 charts the development of this at national level, as well as the flaws that have developed, in the Demos publication *Holistic government* (6, 1997).

At the local level, the steady growth in service provision throughout the century accelerated during the 1950s and 1960s. The 1970s saw major structural reforms with reorganisations across the public services, perhaps most significantly in health and local government. These sought economic and administrative economies of scale by creating far larger organising units with large functional departments within them. However, these functions were largely determined by the growth of professional activity, and (in many cases relatively new) professional organisation, rather than by the logic of either user requirements or service delivery.

There were two linked strands to these reforms. The first was concerned with the geographical levels to be covered by the new hierarchy of tiers to be established and the functions to be covered. The second involved the importation of the then current thinking about better managerial practices from the private sector. These included corporate management, functional management structures, development of personnel departments involving manpower planning, work study, organisation and methods, industrial relations, training, and so on. Perhaps this could be described with hindsight as the start of the new public management version one. In fact, the public services have always experienced the transfer of ideas from the private sector. Sadly, this has frequently been done uncritically and with little regard to either past experience or specific contexts. Further, the public sector seems to take up ideas increasingly past their sell-by dates in the best of the private sector, largely because civil servants are not sufficiently versed in the *range of very different ideologies* that underpin private sector methodologies. They seem obsessed with the outworn Fordist, classical management principles of 'one best way', a top-down blueprint, that by definition excludes learning through practice. Joined-up action simply cannot be planned-in, top-down in this way. This marks a theme to be taken up further in Chapter 5.

There is an irony in that so much of the language of corpacy and top management structures in local government, for example, replicates 'progressive thinking' in the mid-1970s. For instance, the much vaunted Kirklees Model, with policy directors freed from departmental responsibilities, is remarkably similar to that introduced down the road at Bradford and some other authorities in 1974, following the Baines report (DoE, 1972). It is a mistake to assume that many innovations in the public services are quite as new as they seem. This gives a further pointer to the difficulties that the government's emerging new public service agenda will raise. 1970s corpacy, its late 1990s variants, and many of the myriad innovations between, have sought to overcome the silos of departmentalism in the pursuit of joined-up policy and action. The future may need more than old wine in new bottles. The problem being currently described is not a new one – it has been a theme, together with a whole range of potential solutions, throughout the history of public services and from the 1960s onwards in particular.

The effects of increase in scale on the role of political representatives

By the early 1980s, corporate management was rapidly falling into disrepute. There was an increasing desire by many politicians to take firmer control of their authorities at a time of a progressive tightening of budgets and strengthening of central government control. Service directors and chief officers, whatever the original intentions, quickly moved back to the relative comfort of the operational. Politicians became more involved in the operational aspects of delivery. Committee chairs saw it as their role to give direction directly to their services through '*their*' chief officer or director. Chief executives, together with their policy units, found themselves increasingly powerless in the pursuit of corporate policy. Departmentalism, especially in larger authorities, became dominant with elected members increasingly seeing their role as controllers of services, rather than as holders of the economic, social and environmental overview for their districts. Many, it seemed, lost sight of the higher ground and inevitably took many top officers down into the operational swamps with them.

A further consequence of this enlargement in 1974 was to lower the numbers of elected representatives, each councillor representing larger numbers of constituents. Thus Britain has one of the lowest levels of democratic representation in Europe, and perhaps as a consequence of both the scale of local government units and low representation, high levels of public apathy and poor voter turnout (see Rallings and Thrasher, 1996). Elected members have become increasingly unrepresentative of the population as a whole, being disproportionately male, white and over 55 (LGMB's Census of Councillors in England and Wales, reported in the *Local Government Chronicle*, 20 March 1998). This may also be affected by the increasing time demands on part-time councillors because of the sheer scale of the organisations they are attempting to 'manage'. In most places, councils are the largest employer by far in their districts, usually followed a distant second by one or more health trusts. The average councillor, it has been estimated (Young and Rao, 1994), spends 74 hours a month on council business, quite apart from party work. Given the lengthening of the working day for many of those in full-time employment, it is likely that the number of retired and unemployed will rise in the future, unless both the role and the basis of member remuneration is radically changed.

A study of local government councillors conducted in 1993 (Young and Rao, 1994, pp 41-58) found that most were satisfied with their roles, current process of decision making and showed little enthusiasm for change. There is little to suggest that much has changed over the last five years. Given the general tone of the government's recent consultation paper, *Modernising local government* (Democratic Renewal Debate, DETR, 1998), it appears that it may be turning its back on strengthening representative democracy, excepting the pursuit of directly-elected mayors, in favour of consultative mechanisms such as citizens' juries, local focus groups, standing panels and referenda. But at the same time there is a gaining movement to strengthen community-based representation. The London Community Alliance, recently formed and chaired by Lord Young of Dartington, advocates community councils of 10,000 and 15,000 people where one elected member would represent not more than 500 people, "rather than the ratio of 1:3,500 which is the current position, for the London Boroughs" ('Community government', The London Community Alliance, 18 Victoria Park Square, Bethnal Green, London E2 9PF, Tel 0181 980 6263). Outside London, the National Association of Local Councils represents and campaigns for community councils which still cover large parts of England (The National Association of Local Councils, 109 Great Russell Street, London WC1B 3LD, Tel 0171 637 1865). Walsall is pioneering street-based elections to neighbourhood committees (Walsall MBC, 'A story to tell', available from the Chief Executive, Civic Centre, Darwall Street, Walsall WS1 1TP), and the LGMB has developed a thriving local democracy network.

As we show in Chapters 5, 6 and 7, the development of consultative processes can have a major role in the regeneration of both local government and public sector agencies. But there are great dangers that these processes will work within the traditional silos of service provision and departmentalism. As such they would do little to strengthen ties in and between local communities to regenerate so much of the social capital that has been lost over the last 20 years. At worse, the emphasis on service-based 'consumerist' approaches may inadvertently make such capacity building more difficult because they focus on vertical channels of control rather than the lateral linkage between local professionals and emerging community agendas stressed in Chapter 4. We forsake the development of vibrant local communities and networks of democracy at our peril.

Public service reforms in the 1980s and 1990s

The Conservative government of the 1980s and early 1990s became increasingly concerned with both cost and the performance of much of the public services. The waves of reforms they introduced are well documented elsewhere (for example, see Ferlie et al, 1996). But there are three significant aspects to these reforms that have particular relevance for the future of holistic, cross-functional, collaborative action in the future.

Firstly, for the most part, these reforms were aimed at improving the efficiency and performance of services *within* the existing functions. To this extent they tended to reinforce, even more strongly, the functional principle of old.

Secondly, because of the desire to offer choice and improvement, often by trying to mimic private sector market mechanisms, the focus tended to be on short-term efficiencies and outcomes. Therefore, output measures were oriented towards individual consumers and the easily measurable. On the one hand, this has further accentuated the narrowness of departmentalism and the relationship between the individual service provider and individual 'consumers'[1]. But on the other hand, it did provide a much needed focus on outputs, on service users, on what services and delivery units actually cost and how things might be done differently.

Thirdly, the reforms did offer more opportunities through the creation of more devolved units for greater lateral collaboration beyond the clutches of functional control. But the regimes of incentives and penalties tended to reward single service consumer focus. However, there has been a noticeable, even if small and sporadic, growth in such collaborative activity with a focus on both individuals and consumers as beneficiaries of clusters of services. On occasions though, such collaboration conflicts with the demands of functional control and may be seen as deviant behaviour within silo hierarchies even where they espouse the rhetoric of partnership.

Some consequences

Robin Murray, in his seminal article, 'The state after Henry' (1991, pp 22-7) described the organisation of welfare provision of the 1970s as an impure form of the Fordist state. It had grown around the organising principles of automobile mass production and work design methodologies derivative of F.W. Taylor, the founder of modern work study. "The main thrust of Thatcherite policy, inspired by public choice theory, has been to further the Fordist project of the traditional public sector" (Murray, 1991, p 24). The new model, according to Murray's analysis, is based upon an old management model. He then calls for the development of a post-Fordist paradigm.

> **Post-Fordism encourages us to focus on the front line producers of state services, on the users and the relationship between them. (Murray, 1991, p 27)**

The present government, in its desire to reform and recast the delivery of welfare services, would be foolish indeed if it were to underestimate the enormous hold that 'Fordist-type thinking' has in the public services. Many senior managers unwittingly assume the metaphor of organisation as machine. This suggests that organisations can be designed and detailed from the top down and that, like a machine, the whole can be divided into parts and is no more than the sum of the parts. If each person understands their part, role and function in the structure, the system will run like clockwork. Managers become information relays, mainly directed downwards, and fire fighters and troubleshooters, fixing and coordinating when things go wrong or unforeseen problems arise. The focus is upwards and the product/services standardised.

Fordism also easily fits alongside professionally-based 'deficit' models which focus on professionally-determined lacks and needs in clients and therefore underestimate both the actual and potential resources which exist in both individuals and communities. (This theme is taken up in Chapters 3, 4, 5, 6 and 7 and developed.) Deficit models serve to strengthen the hierarchically-dependent relationship between individual client and expert professional helper who attempts to top up the deficit. Similarly, this combination of Fordism and deficit professionalism frequently leads to a parallel disempowering of front-line staff. If there is a problem, then they need training, restructuring, better procedures and protocols. The intelligence and experience of both front-line workers and clients are largely ignored – planners and experts know best.

The post-Fordist paradigm emerged out of the manufacturing revolution led by a number of Japanese car manufacturers – Toyota in particular (see Womack et al, 1990[2]). It was shaped by the very different guiding metaphor of the organisation as a set of interlinking complex systems where improvement came from everybody involved working together to understand and improve the system. Suppliers and customers were seen as part of an organic whole. Dr W. Deming, an American statistician, virtually unknown in the United States until the lasts few years before his death in 1994, had a profound impact when he taught Japanese industrialists the principles of Quality (Deming, 1986[3]). In effect he turned the work study and problem-solving methodologies on their heads by giving workers themselves the tools and the understanding and effectively freeing them from external inspection by staff 'experts'. Both workers and customers were given ownership of their own intelligence. Individual and collective learning became the key to success. It marked a shift from a curative to a preventative culture that in organisational and management terms precisely fits a shift towards preventative government. Without such a shift, progress towards preventative government will remain illusory.

For those interested in the history and ideologies of management, this is both a fascinating and rather depressing story. More immediately, it has significant implications for the pursuit of joined-up action. Western industry had considerable difficulty trying to make the paradigm leap required (see Pascale, 1990). Many found it impossible. In Britain, a reinvigorated car industry has been largely regrown under Japanese ownership. Even now it is widely estimated that 75% of change efforts across the public and private sectors fails to achieve anything other than cosmetic difference[4].

Some of the most specific consequences of this structural and managerial inheritance are addressed briefly below. They are mainly aimed at local government because, if it is to survive as a viable entity into the next century, it will have to take centre stage in much of the change. It is also responsible for a wide range of services. It is, in broad descriptive terms at least, the only multi-service provider and it is the only one under local democratic control. But many of the comments are generalisable, at least in part, to other agencies.

The big silos

This inheritance has meant that health, law and order, education, housing and social services (as well as many other services) are organised in separate silos with different forms of governance as well as cultures, values and employment conditions. Most have little real knowledge of each other's histories, organisations, goals and concerns. Sadly, this is frequently as true between services within local government as between those operating in independent organisations. Professional organisation is also a dominant force. This means that attempted structural solutions rarely produce the hoped-for results. Thus two things can happen. The gaps are simply moved elsewhere and/or the different professional cultures simply will not merge despite structural integration. Attempts to combine housing and social services provide some classic examples of this in local government. In these conditions, promotion is often dependent upon displaying departmental and professional loyalty. Of course there has to be a show of collaboration at coordinating meetings and joint working parties, but for the most part, people are constrained to act as departmental representatives rather than co-colleagues working towards a common picture. People who work closely with other departments or communities are frequently described by service managers 'as going native'.

This should not be taken as meaning that public servants are motivated only by narrow self-interest and their own career interests. Many work valiantly to escape the dominance of the silo cultures. The problem is that it is so easy to get caught up unwittingly into acting out the cultural, thinking and behavioural routines. They are all the more pervasive because they operate at a largely unconscious, taken-for-granted level. Most officers are highly committed to 'good service' but frequently can only see this within the current, usually curative, deficit-based, professional paradigm – and the inevitable first call for more resources. It is these same forces that has made transformation in many private sector organisations so difficult.

But the impact of recent reforms has certainly produced some change in the overall cultural outlook, especially towards performance and greater acknowledgements of service users as customers.

Controlling the pyramid(s)

As the public service silos grew in scale, the attention switched from the wider purposes of the services to their control per se. The progressive growth of scale and size, especially resulting from the 1970s reorganisation, placed an ever-increasing emphasis on controlling – and *defending* – 'the pyramid(s)'. Public disenchantment with services increased as the felt separation of services organisations from their publics grew. Steadily, most public services increasingly lost contact with their publics.

The political, managerial and professional hierarchies struck uneasy compromises over control and territory between bouts of 'readjustment'. In the larger authorities in particular, the trade unions also contested in this power struggle with increasing effectiveness, having learned that the organisation technology of Fordism could be turned to their negotiating advantage. More latterly, the equal opportunities lobby entered the same territory. The focus was almost all internal. Here, all were on common ground.

The postwar expansion saw the increase and development of a wide range of professions and professional bodies. Their power and demarcation lines have become fossilised around the problems, issues, assumptions, and technologies of the 1960s and 1970s. This is perhaps most marked in the health service. The old pyramids and managerial styles are frequently described by critics as 'control and command', but are perhaps better understood – especially in local government – as somewhat unstable coalitions of power.

A shift to holistic, preventative government means that the question of purpose must be held at the forefront, and power used to give over all direction, to enable, to include, to facilitate, rather than become fixated on control[5].

Competition and the myth of the golden past

There is an easy assumption in some quarters that some of the increasingly negative aspects of competitive behaviours, evident across the public services, are a result of the introduction of so-called market mechanisms. This seems to be based on a further assumption that collaboration was the norm before the reforms. This, of course, was simply not the case, despite the post-1974 attempts to introduce corporate planning to bring the whole together. The model was hopelessly functionalist and fell foul of the other contending parties for power.

The development of market mechanisms has been an important spur to change. They challenged poor performance and in its more simplistic forms, made it visible. The downside was that it now apparently legitimised men (and an increasing number of women) behaving badly; it made the worst of defensive, aggressive and non-collaborative behaviour more overt and acceptable. What might have been previously covert could be done because this was how 'market managers' were supposed to behave. One view of market enterprise does emphasise macho, highly competitive, short-term, jungle behaviour. But of course another view from the quality, lean production paradigm favours the very different approach of close collaboration between buyers and suppliers, using competition as a means of being able to 'contest' contracts if collaboration cannot be maintained over the long term[6].

Working towards holistic, preventative government in the future will require that senior managers can work with paradox and dilemmas. Just as they need to seek resolution between top-down and bottom-up, they will also be required to reconcile the collaboration and competition as productive contestability.

The programmatic tendency

Public services are dominated by what can be described as the programmatic approach to change. (Other, systems-based, holistic methodologies are explored in Chapter 4.) Programmatic change naturally assumes the organisation as machine metaphor (the best analysis of the use of metaphor in understanding organisations is in Morgan, 1986). The specific content of a 'change programme' has been described as having some or all of the following characteristics:

1. It is imposed on the organization from the top.

2. **It serves as a centerpiece for launching and driving change throughout the whole organization in the early stages of revitalization.**
3. **Its off-the-shelf standardized solutions are not customized to meet the individual needs of different sub-units.**
4. **Its focus is on one particular human resource management issue: employee skills, leadership style, performance evaluation and compensation, organizational structure, or organizational culture. (Beer et al, 1990, p 36)**

The evidence is that they have little success in producing transformational change (Beer et al, 1990).

The instigators of programmatic change are normally human resources staff or similar, supported by top management. Frequently, though, the latter often have low boredom thresholds, and lose interest after the initial excitement. Rarely are line managers the main agents of change. As the change effort(s) impacts upon them they may find it difficult to see how it answers the real day-to-day problems that they have to address. It may appear as yet another change initiative in an apparently endless series, the meaning of each having long since become detached from the originators' intentions. Programmatic change efforts are often felt to add extra work and not be linked to the main purpose of people's real work. They often become discredited and descend into a kind of mad management disease; endless change programmes being led by different individuals, detached from each other and divorced from any connecting bigger picture. The change effort becomes an end in itself; another task to be done, a box ticked; or quietly forgotten, when top management has lost interest and moved on to the next fad. Sadly, nearly all quality initiatives suffer the same fate.

Each change programme is likely to bring with it a new language. For instance, quality programmes are likely to advocate the virtues of listening to and involving staff, teamwork and so on. But the medium for the delivery of the message will often be manuals, training programmes and top-down briefing – processes at odds with the message. Thus what is evidently good practice in other arenas will be greeted with increasing scepticism. People learn a new language to be used in appropriate formal settings while maintaining their old behaviours, which see them through 'in the real world'.

An important feature of the programmatic approach is the way in which change philosophies, which came out of organic and systems-based paradigms, are 'packaged' into the machine paradigm. This is, of course, just as much an infliction in the private sector. The Quality philosophy, approach and methods developed by Deming and others was recast as TQM (total quality management) and numerous other packaged manifestations. A whole new bureaucracy sprang up around firstly, BS5750 and more latterly ISO9000, and a gamut of audit-type approaches based upon endless paperwork, procedures and verification. John Seddon, a British writer and consultant in the Deming tradition, has produced perhaps the most vigorous critique of ISO9000 (Seddon, 1997). His 10-point summary is reproduced in Box 3 below. He describes the latest variant, QS9000 as "ISO9000 on steroids".

Box 3: John Seddon's 10-point summary against ISO9000

1. ISO9000 encourages organisations to act in ways that make things worse for their customers.
2. Quality by inspection is not quality.
3. ISO9000 starts from the flawed presumption that work is best controlled by specifying the controlling procedures.
4. The typical method of implementation is bound to cause suboptimisation of performance.
5. The Standard relies too much on people's and particularly assessors' interpretation of quality.
6. The Standard promotes, encourages, and explicitly demands actions that cause suboptimisation.
7. When people are subjected to external controls, they will be inclined to pay attention only to those things that are affected by the controls.
8. ISO9000 has discouraged managers from learning about the theory of variation.
9. ISO9000 has failed to foster good customer–supplier relations.
10. As an intervention, ISO9000 has not encouraged managers to think differently.

This appealed to the machine thinkers, but completely missed the point. Quality had been appropriated back into the top-down inspection, Fordist paradigm. Deming taught of continuous improvement by all working together; of eliminating unnecessary waste, of everybody inspecting their own work and ending the necessity for end-of-the-line, top-down inspection. He urged prevention rather than cure.

It is unlikely that public services will have much success in moving towards outward-looking, holistic, preventative, community enhancing services until they are able to embrace and develop change methodologies appropriate to the task. Of course, public service organisations, like all other organisations, require order and control. But they also need to work with change and flux. It should not be the case of either/or. It is another dilemma to be accepted and reconciled.

The public service 'infrastructure'

We have inherited a set of structures, professions, skill mixes and job demarcations which have emerged as a series of responses to the needs of a society and its conditions, technologies and politics, that have long since passed. Despite the efforts of previous Conservative governments, this remains largely unchanged. If it were possible to start again with a greenfield site, it is inconceivable that we would create anything like the same organisational and professional architecture we now have.

Inevitably a whole array of institutional infrastructure has expanded around similar fault lines and underlying assumptions. This is both a result of the functional inheritance and serves to consolidate it.

Managerial and professional journals, for the most part, keep within the territory of the major silos. Academic departments follow a similar course, as do professional bodies and employers' organisations. Whatever limited linkages there may be across the main professions and silos, the theory and practice of community development remains almost completely beyond the pale.

These fractures help to maintain the status quo and seriously limit the arenas where holistic, preventative methodologies can be developed which link action, learning and theory. Since the onset of public sector reforms in the mid-1980s, there has been a sharp increase in the quantity of theorising about the "new public management". But much of this is limited by narrow interpretations of private sector management theory and practice. The assumption is frequently made that there is a single widely accepted model, rather than the very different paradigms that actually exist. Public services are different and must pursue their own path, say many of the new public management theorists, neatly pulling up the drawbridge between the public sector and more radical private sector ideas. This also unwittingly helps to provide the intellectual underpinning for the repackaging of systems-based change methodologies into apparently more contextualised public sector *programmes* and thus back into the quasi-Fordist paradigm, simply adding more bells and whistles.

There are parallel processes at work in the way public service clients seek external help from consultancies and academic establishments[7]. They like to employ people who are credible to them and highly knowledgeable ('expert') about the *context* of current issues. The expert needs to be worldly enough to provide outside legitimisation, while remaining sufficiently close to the client system to avoid unduly threatening it. This may also be a reason for the recycling of increasing numbers of high profile managers into leading consultancies and public service academic departments. This serves to promote the illusion of change, while ensuring that thinking and action remains limited to modifications within the current paradigm.

The implications of organisational change and learning

It would be difficult to provide a better, or more succinct, description of the current state of much of local government in particular, than that provided by Schon's quotation which starts this chapter. The implications for a reforming government are both profound and awkward.

The likely reaction by delivery agencies will be to take each *item* of change separately and attempt to respond to each by absorbing it into the status quo; a new policy here, an extra unit there and so on. Programmatic approaches depend upon 'planning change in' from the top down. While this may require new routines and skills, it does not essentially involve people learning to do things radically differently, especially in relation to the outside world. The focus is entirely on the individual and not upon the connections between them; learning becomes private (privatised) rather than public. Similarly, each item of the external threat is picked off and dealt with individually. Thus individuals may learn (and get increasingly frustrated) but organisations do not.

Therefore the government should 'intervene' in this 'dynamic conservatism' by placing the focus of change outside the formal organisation of public service agencies and institutions and into 'the community'. They will need to continue to develop a range of incentives and penalties in support of this. In particular, they will have to ensure that holistic outcome measures are established, especially through the BestValue initiatives that are very clearly linked to *community* involvement and capacity building. The status quo will readily focus on threats to internal and known procedures. Debates over elected mayors, cabinet-style government, new election processes and so on, will be grist to the mill, becoming steadily more technical and divorced from the initial problems that the reforms sought to address. While discussion and debate is obviously necessary, it may well take attention away from the bigger picture of change and especially from the even more threatening community governance agenda. These reforms do have something to recommend them, but government ministers will need to keep the focus on the bigger picture, on holistic, preventative government, and most importantly of all, on and into the communities they seek to transform.

Thus, there are two broad dangers with the government's range of proposed change initiatives, especially as they apply to local government. Firstly, each will be dealt with as an item in itself, irrespective of the original intentions or how it fits with the other initiatives or with the government's overall intentions. Each will then become a disconnected project driven by programmatic management. Secondly, and consequently, the bigger picture is lost and the projects add to overload. Everything does get implemented after a fashion, but yet everything stays more or less the same, at least so far as joined-up action is concerned. Local government has become too task mesmerised. Much of it seems to say, 'we proved we could do it under the last government. We will implement all this lot too. Just tell us what to do'. But what was the problem in the first place? Unless this is kept to the fore, the new stream of initiatives in total may produce further deterioration. The problem is not so much in the initiatives, or the broad intentions, it will be in the implementation. Working harder, but in the same way, will *not* produce radical change.

Notes

[1] References to consumers and consumerist approaches refer to a focus on the relationship between individual service users and/or beneficiaries. They may or may not make a payment for all or part of the cost of the service. Also they may have little power of choice or exit. It is a term that is in widespread use in the public services but it may have rather different implications and consequences when compared with the use of the term in private sector settings. However, it is useful in distinguishing between a focus on the individual and on the citizen. This is developed further in Chapter 6, particularly in relation to the development of Best Value. While 'service user' and the 'beneficiaries' are probably better terms, 'consumer' does suggest a higher status (or just professional patronage?); that people should be accorded the dignity and rights *as though they had* a real consumer choice.

[2] Womack et al, 1990, describe the Japanese-led challenges to the mass

production in the car industry and the development of 'lean production'. They also chronicle the difficulties of Western manufacturers to even understand the paradigm shift in thinking and action, let alone learn and implement it.

[3] This was his most significant book. His work has been developed by many other practitioners, consultants and academics. Further information can be obtained from the British Deming Association, 25 Water Lane, Salisbury, Wiltshire SP2 7TE, Tel 01722 412138. There has, in recent years, been an increasing interest in systems, systems thinking and self-organising. See reference to Morgan, 1986. Also Senge, 1990. This has also renewed interest in the work of Gregory Bateson, whose work traversed anthropology, psychiatry, biological evolution, genetics, systems theory and ecology. See Bateson, 1972. For a current exploration of these broad themes in an increasingly interconnected world see Mulgan, 1997.

[4] For instance, see Kennedy and Harvey (1997) who quote from a US study where only a third of major change efforts across 500 US companies had any significant positive effect. The figure of 75% failure accords with the research studies drawn on in this report. Similarly Business Intelligence reports suggest similar levels of failure in attempts to install widespread corporate change through TQM and Business Process Reengineering. [Background information and further references can be obtained from Peter Hawkins, Bath Consultancy Group, 24 Gay Street, Bath BA1 2PD.]

[5] Fixation on control is usually an outcome of a zero-sum perception of power. Power is limited and becomes dissipated if not narrowly protected. Either I have it, or you do. If I share it with you I lose control. This issue is discussed further, as well as its alternatives in Chapter 8, pp 142-3.

[6] See Ham, 1996. Ham uses the term 'contestability' to describe such collaborative arrangements where competition can still exist. For a history of the development of collaborative buyer/supplier relations in the car industry – and the enormous thinking and behaviour shifts this required – see Womack et al, 1990.

[7] The reservation about making a stronger statement about this is because it is impressionistic only. The writers know of no research into this. It would be a useful and potentially revealing study.

THREE

The public service, community interface

**We have just had our bid to the SRB Challenge Fund approved.
Where do we go from here in involving the community?
(DoE, 1995, p 5)**

**Those concerned with democracy and development ... should
be building a more civic community, but they should lift
their sights beyond instant results.... Building social capital
will not be easy, but it is the key to making democracy work.
(Putnam, 1993, p 185)**

This chapter focuses primarily on issues and questions that have arisen
during work involving community development and regeneration,
particularly the extent to which this is helped or hindered by the work
of public service institutions and delivery agencies. It has been these
experiences that led to the wider questions asked and issues raised in
this report, and provided the stimulus to propose alternative ways forward.

The above quote is taken from an excellent 'practitioners' guide' to
regeneration produced by the former Department of the Environment
(DoE). But it reflects, probably inadvertently, the ambivalence that
surrounds both the nature and status of communities and the reasons
for involving them. The assumption in the statement above is that
ownership of the bid has been firmly with the institutions, but that
there now needs to be some kind of participation. But for what purpose?

The research evidence shows that there are two fundamental
requirements for the achievement of sustainable regeneration. Firstly,
there needs to be a strengthening of social cohesion to overcome the
social fragmentation, isolation and lack of self-esteem that so often exists.
This provides the capacity to sustain high levels of involvement built
around local agendas. Secondly, mainstream service spending and delivery
needs to be attuned to work in partnership, both with each other, and

the community, in pursuit of local needs and agendas. In effect, special regeneration monies can provide short-term additional funds to promote and facilitate these developments. But they can just as easily divert attention *away* from the crucial need to address patterns of, and links between, mainstream spending. These topics are covered more fully in Chapter 4.

It is evident that this research has had some impact upon public policy. There has been increasing stress placed on local consultation and community involvement. Recent government consultation specifically raises the issue of community capacity building (DETR, 1997). However, there seems to be uncertainty about the purpose of this and whether it is little more than extended consultation. There is no analysis of the nature of the relationship between institutions, service providers and the community(ies) and how this should change.

Despite this ambivalence, the last government signalled a positive move towards more holistic approaches by creating the Single Regeneration Budget (SRB) Challenge Fund (bringing previously independent funding regimes into one pool) and establishing regional government offices. But it seems that for all the rhetoric of partnership, involvement and empowerment contained in policy statements, reality on the ground, at the level of neighbourhoods and estates, is often very different. Given the programmatic tendency described in the last chapter, it is possible to both predict and understand many of the problems that can and do occur during implementation once funds have been 'won'. It is these problems that lessen the chances of achieving longer-term sustainability.

How bidding processes and the construction of projects works against sustainable change

How does this come about? Take, for instance, the bidding process for SRB. Typically a group of top officials with local executive authority will come together and declare the existence of a partnership. This may involve elected members. Under this formal leadership, groups of officers will start to assemble projects that fit both the criteria laid out in the SRB policy and match up to *their* perception of local need. There will often be some level of consultation on various projects conducted by different local project teams. However, tight deadlines for submission mean that the different projects are constructed in isolation both from each other, and from informed community perspectives. At the same time, such community activity that does exist is frequently fractured, ad hoc and unconnected with little capacity for either self or external coordination. Thus neighbourhoods or communities are not able to plan or engage in any wider processes around their assessments of need. The organising logic is that of the professional deficit model (see p 32).

Further, SRB rules – the reasonable requirement to get value for public money and to ensure that the money is spent on what it is meant to be spent on – require that projects have detailed measurable outputs and deadlines. These then have to be met in order that further money is released.

From a civil service perspective (and to a degree senior officers' perspective in local agencies) this makes eminent sense. Further, everyone wants value for money, especially those in the deprived areas, with the possible exception of the usually very small criminal/disruptive element. However, the typical SRB process and outcomes are likely to have a number of unintended consequences.

- Once the money has been 'won', the 'partnership' signatories often believe that their main task has been done. What remains is a relatively simple implementation task.
- Similarly, the relevant regional government office is likely to see its task as monitoring the 'partnership' to ensure that the delivery plan is adhered to and that *hard data is collected to prove it.*
- Because of the lack of soft 'process measures', the key elements of capacity building tend to be ignored. What is concentrated on is what can be measured easily rather than what is important. This is an urgent priority for further research.
- All this is likely to happen with little connection to the mainstream spend of service delivery and related activity in the relevant areas. For example, community safety is likely to be an issue, but it is often difficult for agencies to agree action based on the links between tenancy agreements, housing management policy, neighbourhood watches and local policing methods. What is often obvious to local citizens (including those frequently categorised as the underclass) about addressing the causal connections required to deal with the severely disruptive minority, is not so apparent in the individual agencies.
- There is often a good deal of anger from local people about attempts to consult and/or involve them. This may be both because of the traditional dependency relationship with providers, as well as the perception that everything has been decided anyway. Because 'consultation' is now a prerequisite for so many funding regimes, there is often a kind of 'consultation fatigue' on the ground. The

feeling is that officers are just going through the motions for pet schemes that they will do anyway. People are far more 'cute' about professional rituals than are many of the professionals themselves.

- What was meant to be 'empowering' becomes disempowering, fostering greater cynicism and dependency. Some regeneration projects have 'swept' into local neighbourhoods and cut straight across already fragile community networks, rather like some well-intentioned colonising project. *While there has been increasing emphasis of exit strategies, little is said about entry strategies which are critical to success.*
- Thus, means become short-term ends in themselves and the big picture is lost – and often the communities become further disconnected. Any focus on 'institutional change' is lost in the flurry of activity. Meanwhile, members and senior officers feel good because they have 'won resources' for necessary and worthwhile objectives. But, because the different parties inhabit such different social and professional worlds, this dislocation of effort and intention can go unseen for many years. Those at the top of the agencies – 'the partners' – and the government office want/need to hear good news so care is taken to ensure that this is what is heard and the concentration on hard measures makes this easier. Narrow programmatic management is applied to each disconnected project. (More action research is required to enable longer-term learning about the sustainability of individual projects and their appropriate linkage into others. We need to know during the lifetime of a renewal scheme whether even short-term outputs survive – especially building and external physical improvements.)

Further forces maintaining the status quo

There are further pressures that increase the tendencies for these top-down, machine-like interventions.

Firstly, the variety of projects and the different professional backgrounds tend to keep most professionals locked into their own worlds of different cultures, assumptions, priorities and organisational and governance structures. There are few real opportunities for them to make sense of each other's realities and forge new collective meaning together as well as with emerging community structures and representations. Committee-type meetings, with tight agendas, remote from 'front-line' contact, held in civic palaces, are rarely adequate. Because of the frequent lack of adequate partnership leadership, the silo obstacles to front-line partnering remain untouched.

Secondly, the pressure and volume of the waves of public sector reforms have placed great emphasis on top-down change, short-term outputs, external audit and 'competitive' behaviour. Certainly there was a need for many of the changes with better accountability for the stewardship of public resources and a much clearer focus on results. Even where there is both obvious need and policy rhetoric for people to work together, it is often difficult to get them into the same room together. When they do, 'the game' is often to use the superficialities of managerially correct language – including collaboration – while indulging in further destructive and narrowly competitive (defensive) behaviour behind closed doors. Of course, health would be a leading example here. However, elected members will frequently use their democratic mandate and their control of officers in equally narrow ways.

Thirdly, as described above, the importation and interpretation of private sector organisational and managerial practices frequently operate at a very simplistic and naive level. What were often holistic, systemic ideas in origin are converted into streams of pragmatic, top-down interventions, usually resting upon structure change, procedure writing and mechanistic training. Where real change does happen, it usually owes more to the talent of creative and inventive local leadership or because people are simply fearful of the future.

There are great dangers that unless these issues are addressed, Best Value may inadvertently accentuate this fragmentation by focusing on the suboptimisation of the parts (service/departmental/professionally driven) at the expense of the overall effectiveness of the whole (see Chapter 7). Will service improvement proceed from whole system perspectives with the bigger picture in mind – where communities and beneficiaries *together* with service providers work towards effectiveness? Or will holistic notions like continuous improvement be dragged into a mechanistic framework of 'command and control' where spurious efficiency savings are sought in 'the parts' in isolation from, at the expense of, the whole. The current low level of organisational capacity for working with people in much of local government does not auger well. There is a high orientation towards the hard factors such as structures, procedures and finance and usually little to the 'soft' (actually they are the harder to do) areas of developing cross-boundary teams of committed people. Despite the frequent references to culture change, learning organisations, and partnership, local government in particular remains a desert when it comes to using the tools of change management.

Fourthly, because of the above, there is often a failure to see all the services, institutions, citizens and communities as inhabiting the same system, the same world – although they are experienced as very different worlds. Often few, if any, are holding the continually changing bigger picture. There is then no catalyst for enabling ever increasing numbers of others to do the same so that they can implement their past with colleagues who all have the whole in mind.

Fragmentation, power and powerlessness

Many current systems on the ground are characterised by the fragmentation of effort. Despite this there is considerable effort and good practice, but so much of it is disconnected. This seriously decreases the potential for collective improvement and in particular, for learning. This fragmentation may be viewed from three perspectives:

- firstly, fragmentation within and across the institutions and agencies;
- secondly, ambiguity about the meaning and practice of consultation and involvement at the interface between agencies and their 'public';
- thirdly, fragmentation within and across communities themselves.

Fragmentation within and across agencies

Across a district[1] it is often possible to find numerous initiatives of closer working with communities but nearly all conducted from the silos and frequently unknown to each other. Tenant participation exercises, schools working with parents on better reading schemes, day care schemes for elderly people, community social work, capacity building initiatives and community policy, may all be operating across the same geographical patch, largely or wholly unknown to each other. Working together, there should be plenty of synergy and a focus on whole communities. This fragmentation of effort, on the other hand, tends to lead to working with individuals as users of single services, whatever the declared intentions. And this will usually fail to make much overall impact on the dependency relations between providers and users or to strengthen communities.

Similarly, a local authority and district partnership groups will often have experience of a number of recent and current regeneration schemes. But again there is usually little connection of effort or learning either within the district or beyond. Each becomes as isolated as the agencies themselves. And with SRB, the parts are distributed back into and across the individual silos themselves.

This starts to raise some important questions about the challenges posed by the development of the new action zones for health, education and employment, as well as other initiatives, including Best Value pilots, which have a multi-agency/community focus, better government for older people, healthy living centres and so on.

- To what extent will they enhance what is already known about effective locally-based partnership learning? (Learning from existing knowledge.)
- How will different projects learn from each other, and how will this learning be made available on a wider basis?
- How will those involved draw upon the extensive empirical data of successful sustainable working, rather than concentrating on endless wheel reinvention? (See Chapter 4.)
- To what extent will new ways of working in the specific geographical area or client groupings be developed across whole districts on a multi-agency basis? Or will they just be seen as specific one-off projects to combat disadvantage?
- Will they be seen as opportunities for agencies to move from dependent/deficiency relationships over communities, towards interdependence, partnership around community agendas, and rebuilding community linkages?
- Or will there be increasingly overlapping, uncoordinated and unthinking consultation exercises at local levels designed more to enact the tick box requirements of government agencies and funding bodies (with the consequences of increasing the anger and frustration of those who live such difficult lives in distressed and poor communities)?

Consultation and involvement: the ambiguity of learning and practice

The causes of the anger and frustration often experienced by many of the supposed beneficiaries of these processes have been described above. Given the government's stated intentions to work towards community improvement and reformed local governance, it will need to clarify what this terminology implies in both meaning and action.

In some situations, current practice on the ground, despite the rhetoric, intensifies frustration and fragmentation of effort. There are obvious dangers, despite the opposite intentions, that the new wave of top-down initiatives may simply add to this. This is, of course, not for the most part because the initiatives are misplaced; it is critically an issue about implementation and time scales. Because social decay and deprivation has been taking place over many years, it will take many years to build up the community capacity to sustain regeneration. This is what the evidence suggests (see Chapter 4, and the following section).

The matrix developed in Chapter 7 (pp 135-6) is designed to clarify the differences as well as the overlaps across a range of styles of interactions between services and communities. These issues are of particular relevance to the development of Best Value.

Fragmentation across communities

Communities can be thought of in a number of different ways. Most commonly in this report we are referring to communities of place – however difficult to define these are in practice, being dependent upon sometimes competing local perceptions. In addition to communities of place, we can also think in terms of communities of ethnicity, faith, occupation and interest. And communities of interest can be of different sorts:
- recreation and leisure (clubs etc)
- age/stage (mothers, older people, carers, health etc)
- pressure groupings (action groups etc)
- mutual aid.

Linked to these different forms of community, there exists an extraordinary range and diversity of voluntary activity, glimpses of which are illustrated in Chapter 6. However, much of it remains fragmented and isolated against a background of deteriorating social cohesion and in comparison with the scale and resources of the institutions and agencies. This is well illustrated by Barry Knight and Peter Stokes,

> **Part of the weakness of civil society today lies in the narrow sectarianism and splintering of community interests. In any large British city there are perhaps fifty charities working in the field of housing and homelessness. There are as many each working on drug abuse, environmental issues or disability. There will be scores of women's groups and ethnic minority organisations. There are many hundreds of tenants and residents associations, all facing the same problems but they never speak with one powerful voice. Narrow, sectional**

interests, whether these are based on gender, race, geography, or particular issues and causes are always weak, marginalised, easy to buy off and overrule. Much local (and national) politics is about appeasing small vocal interest groups at a local or section level (a play scheme here, a zebra crossing there) in order to disguise and divide broader shared interests. (Knight and Stokes, nd, p 15)

It is against this background that much local authority practice, regeneration bidding processes and delivery mechanisms, together with the funding regimes of the National Lottery, inadvertently accentuate feelings of powerlessness.

Power and powerlessness

When presented with the evidence of need, social dislocation and deprivation, public service leaders are likely themselves to experience feelings of powerlessness. In the face of central controls and restrictions, overloaded managerial and political agendas, unwieldy organisations, lack of spare resources not already tied up in staffing budgets or priority tasks, they feel helpless to respond. The temptation must be to keep up the barriers and avoid the pain[2].

On the other hand, faced with articulate, powerful resource holders, community leaders feel equally powerless to create any changes in institutional behaviour which from their perspective often make little sense. Each side sees the other as powerful and demanding while feeling powerless itself.

Box 4: The disintegration of neighbourhood trust

In some areas trust in neighbours has all but disappeared. In one study conducted for Newcastle City Challenge by Blake Stevenson Ltd, residents described one area as a 'War Zone'. Burglaries, car crime, violence, threatening behaviour, all night parties, drunkenness in the street were the norm. Problems were caused by a minority of 29 residents from 13 families who together possessed 395 criminal convictions. Sixty Asian households were the first to leave, but others followed suit. One young family called the police after their fourth burglary. Minutes after the panda car had left, all the windows in the house were smashed. This family fled the area, for the sake of their mental health, leaving behind a house that was virtually valueless despite it having a £25,000 mortgage.

When crime attacks civil society in this manner almost all 'social capital' is destroyed. People can think no bigger than dealing with their immediate problems, adopt a siege mentality, and withdraw from the public stage. Efforts to rebuild civil society in this particular area, seen as a pre-condition of investing in the local economy, led to a successful public meeting, but it was noteworthy that the only way people could be persuaded to come to the meeting was through hiring 10 security guards to patrol the area while the meeting was going on. Their role was to watch for burglaries and to protect the people walking to and from the meeting.

There are 40 areas in Britain which justify the label of 'no-go' area, where civil society has collapsed, and people live in fear. Such observations are not confined to areas traditionally considered poor. Bradley Stoke is a privately owned housing village designed to be a 'community with a difference – free of crime and problems associated with inner cities'. The reality has proved different with high crime, ram-raiding incidents, and apathy among residents. There is a total lack of civic engagement. It proved impossible to sell 100 tickets to a community event while the 12,000 locals complain that there is nothing to do. (Knight and Stokes, 1996)

And yet there is so much evidence that says that of all these same resources, together with the potential of so many people – both professionals, workers and citizens – could be more effectively used, the whole system can be unblocked and sustainable improvements made. But in an increasing number of areas of Britain the task has become increasingly daunting.

Maintenance of these vicious cycles of decay preserve the interests of those who benefit from criminality and lawlessness as well as those who jealously preserve the status quo in support of their professional, political and managerial power bases. Changing the status quo requires collaboration of all these parties, the powerful and powerless. For the powerful – for all their feelings of powerlessness when confronted with change – the challenge is to risk the uncertainty of the unknown, real learning and redefining the nature of their professionalism and the managerial task.

The relationship between civic society and good governance

So far this chapter has looked at some significant features of the interfaces between communities and public service agencies and institutions, largely in the context of attempts towards regeneration. Robert Putnam has provided some challenging and provocative conclusions about the relationship between the success and effectiveness of democratic institutions and the strength of 'civic community' which surround them. They are, as it were, part of one whole, with the inevitable implication that to develop institutions and/or communities must be addressed from an holistic perspective. The relationship between them is central to improvement.

In *Making democracy work: Civic traditions in modern Italy*, Putnam reports on a 20-years plus intensive, empirical study of the development of regional government since 1970 in Italy, undertaken by himself and colleagues (Putnam, 1993). This book, particularly its final chapter on social capital and institutional success, should be essential reading for policy makers and those leading institutional and agency change – despite some who might be tempted to question what on earth civic traditions in modern Italy have got to do with Cleckhuddersfax.

The central finding is that the success of the new institutions could largely have been predicted from the levels of civic community existing in the regions; high levels of success relating directly to the existence of strong civic traditions going back over a thousand years. "... History suggests that *both* states *and* markets operate more efficiently in civic settings" (Putnam, 1993, p 181). This is challenging news for government reformers, seeking to create or reform democratic institutions, often in the absence of well-established civic communities and networks. In Britain, it also suggests that if we want reinvigorated local institutions linked to a strengthened local and regional democracy, then in the long term this will be dependent upon maintaining and strengthening the bonds of civic engagement and social trust.

Much of Putnam's analysis is based upon the success or otherwise of reconciling the dilemmas of collective – or collaborative – action. Where this is absent, transaction and enforcement costs are high or unworkable, frequently mitigating against any agreement to trade or exchange. Where trust is low, the person who makes the first move towards, or gesture of, cooperation can expect to be left with the 'sucker's pay off'. Not to trust can be rational given the context. Box 5 illustrates a number of these classic archetypal dilemmas. It is easy to translate these into the context of community breakdowns described by Knight and Stokes above, as well as to relationships between agencies (when community care breaks down, attempts to externalise costs to other agencies and over zealous short-term contracting in health, for example) and between agencies and communities.

Box 5: Dilemmas of collective action

Robert Putnam starts with the original "dilemma that confounds rational public spiritedness" in the parable by David Hume, the 18th-century Scottish philosopher. "Your corn is ripe to-day; mine will be so to-morrow. 'Tis profitable for us both, that I shou'd labour with you to-day, and that you shou'd aid me to-morrow. I have no kindness for you, and know you have as little for me. I will not, therefore, take any pains upon your account; and should I labour with you upon my own account, in expectation of a return, I know I shou'd be disappointed, and that I shou'd in vain depend upon your gratitude. Here then I leave you to labour alone; You treat me in the same manner. The seasons change; and both of us lose our harvests for want of mutual confidence and security."

He then goes on to describe four archetypal predicaments studied by game theorists.

- In *the tragedy of the commons*, no herder can limit grazing by anyone else's flock. If he limits his own use of the common meadow, he alone loses. Yet unlimited grazing destroys the common resource on which the livelihood of all depends.

- A *public good*, such as clean air or safe neighborhoods, can be enjoyed by everyone, regardless of whether he contributes to its provision. Under ordinary circumstances, therefore, no one has an incentive to contribute to providing the public good, and too little is produced, causing all to suffer.

- In the dismal *logic of collective action*, every worker would benefit if all struck simultaneously, but whoever raises the strike banner risks betrayal by a well-rewarded scab, so everyone waits, hoping to benefit from someone else's foolhardiness.

- In *the Prisoner's Dilemma*, a pair of accomplices is held incommunicado, and each is told that if he alone implicates his partner, he will escape scot-free, but if he remains silent, while his partner confesses, he will be punished especially severely. If both remained silent, both would be let off lightly, but unable to coordinate their stories, each is better off squealing, *no matter what the other does*. (Putnam, 1993, pp 163-4)

Overcoming dilemmas of collective action and the vicious cycles of individual opportunism and short-termism they produce "depends on the broader social context within which any particular game is played. Voluntary co-operation is easier in a community that has inherited a substantial stock of social capital." (Putnam, 1993, p 167).

Social capital "refers to features of social organisation, such as trust, norms, and networks, that can improve the efficiency of society by facilitating co-ordinated actions." (Putnam, 1993, p 167). It is a result of people participating in many kinds of civic activity, sports clubs, leisure activities, business networks, pressure groups, mutual aid societies, community groups and so on. Through this people experience 'generalised' reciprocity where a benefit experienced now will be repaid at some time in the future. This applies not just within known familiar relationships, but becomes a broad expectation about developing relationships with strangers. It is 'weak' ties of this latter type spread across many relationships and boundaries that nourish wider cooperation. Social capital, according to Putnam, is undervalued and as such, taken for granted. On the other hand, its lack can be very evident, and be difficult to create.

A further strong feature of civic societies is that they are based on strong *horizontal* networks of collaboration that are held together by virtuous cycles of reciprocity and trust. In contrast very uncivic societies are more likely to be held together by vertical networks and supplication; patronage and protectionism offered by higher authority, legal or beyond the law, become the best protection against neighbours (or those in other organisations) who cannot be trusted. In these conditions, societies are held together by vicious cycles of dependence and exploitation.

> **A vertical network, no matter how dense and no matter how important to its participants, cannot sustain social trust and co-operation. Vertical flows of information are often less reliable than horizontal flows, in part because the subordinate husbands information as a hedge against exploitation. More important sanctions that support norms of reciprocity against the threat of opportunism are less likely to be imposed upwards and less likely to be acceded to, if imposed. Only a bold or foolhardy subordinate lacking ties of solidarity with peers, would seek to punish a superior. (Putnam, 1993, p 174)**

Hierarchical and dependent relationships are at best 'lopsided' or asymmetrical and threaten to destabilise horizontal relationships. It is evident, of course, that all forms of human collaboration and institutions involve both vertical and horizontal relationships, even the most participative of organisations. Further, it is almost always a cruel deception, especially in more formal organisations when leaders say that all have equal voices and that hierarchy does not exist. The important question here is, of course, the balance between the two; the extent to which formal authority is seen as legitimate, legal, accountable and transparent, and is used to give direction, leadership and support to the horizontal ties of the wider civic society. It is the horizontal networks of civic society that give this legitimacy to vertical authority. It in turn needs to foster this by serving to strengthen its source. This is a continuing theme through the report.

Putnam's work illustrates that good governance is an outcome of high levels of civicness that support the growth of social capital. But can change also work in the reverse direction? Putnam's answer seems to be a limited yes, "*that changing formal institutions can change political practice*" (Putnam, 1993, p 184). Reforms can produce "a more moderate, pragmatic, tolerant elite political culture" which in turn helps to increase levels of lateral connectedness and thus social capital. He concludes that, "Those concerned with democracy and development ... should be building a more civic community, but they should lift their sights beyond instant results.... Building social capital will not be easy, but it is the key to making democracy work" (Putnam, 1993, p 185).

The next two chapters on change that works review empirical evidence that suggests ways in which institutions can work to develop social capital, especially where current stocks are low through social capacity building. It also shows how they need to manage themselves if they are to direct, guide and support this.

Notes

[1] The term 'district' is used fairly loosely here. It generally means a geographical area considerably larger than local neighbourhoods. Districts can be thought of as approximately the size of parliamentary constituencies, local authority boundaries, or overlapping several such boundaries, particularly for small authorities.

[2] This was well illustrated in the 'Powerful Whispers' project in Bradford, the early stages of what was to become the C2M project described in Chapter 6, pp 112-18. An account of 'Powerful Whispers' is available from Elaine Appelbee at 168 Highfield Lane, Keighley, West Yorkshire BD21 2HU.

FOUR

Change that works – sustaining community and quality of life improvement

One of the most depressing aspects of the study of urban regeneration is the incidence of wheel reinvention, and the failure properly to absorb the lessons of experience ... there have been the 5-volume ESRC study on urban economic development, the 70 papers generated between 1987 and 1993 by the Inner Cities Task Force Initiative, the DoE's Inner Cities Research series; and a substantial research programme in Scotland, commissioned by the Scottish Office, Scottish Enterprise and Scottish Homes. Yet there is little evidence that practitioners or policy makers learn from all this. (Fordham, 1995, p 30)

In the context of what has been written so far, perhaps the failure to learn is hardly surprising. It is this insularity – the 'not-invented-here' syndrome – that is at the core of the corporate amnesia of much of local government in particular and service delivery agencies in general. Essentially, the new public service agenda requires systemic understanding and action from organisations whose dominant cultures and mental maps are from a different world. Certainly there are many examples where people have innovated against the grain but this is frequently difficult and sometimes contentious within the organisations themselves. This is all the more paradoxical when such innovation follows apparently stated policy. The rhetoric of change and partnership frequently outruns the reality of experience.

Changing the cultures and structures of public service organisations to meet the new agenda will be a formidable task. To approach this, it is necessary to understand some of the key processes involved in change that works. This will be done here from two linked perspectives. Firstly, from the more external focus of sustainable community change and development and secondly, from an internal focus of organisational transformation. From these understandings it is possible to start on the task of constructing a series of recommendations to establish other levers and frameworks capable of enabling public service delivery bodies to make the cultural leap that in so many cases will be necessary.

Sustainable community building

It is now widely recognised that the weakening of community and social bonds of cohesion is inextricably linked with the problems of poor health, unemployment, social disadvantage and poverty. Further, the rebuilding of this cohesion, or social capital, is the stated aim of many regeneration interventions. In many cases, however, the rhetoric may add up to little of long-term consequence on the ground. What needs to be recognised is that the causes of both urban and rural disadvantage are systemic and multi-faceted and have developed over many years – in many cases over several decades. Thus it is likely that any stabilising or reversal of these conditions will also take a substantial period. But much of the regeneration effort of recent years has been underpinned by the philosophy of targeted quick hits which is likely to run counter to facilitating the building of local capacity capable of sustaining these changes.

The case for 'community involvement' and 'partnership' appears to have been largely won but what this means in practice – the how – is rather more elusive. But, despite these difficulties and the wide-scale failure to learn from the research, there is a wealth of positive experience to draw upon. The most comprehensive analysis is drawn from the work supported by the Joseph Rowntree Foundation and summarised by Marilyn Taylor in *Unleashing the potential: Bringing residents to the centre of regeneration* (Taylor, 1995). There is also much other material. (Taylor, 1995, draws upon 33 studies to reach her conclusions and these are listed in Appendix A of her report, pp 85-100; these are also the studies referred to and referenced in Fordham, 1995. Two further studies are worthy of particular note: Power, 1997 and Power and Tunstall, 1995.)

It was estimated that there were at least 2,000 large unpopular housing estates in Britain in 1994 (Power, 1994) and that the inequalities that help to give rise to them have been increasing. The lessons learned from the research are applicable to increasing areas of the country. But many of the findings resonate increasingly with the need to strengthen local communities far beyond the dangerous stereotyping of deprived urban estate social housing.

The key messages and themes are as follows.

Poverty and exclusion: Not surprisingly, poverty is at the root of many of the problems experienced by local residents. This in turn leads to disconnections from wider social networks beyond the immediate locality. Frequently there is discrimination by postal code. Potentially unstable social conditions may be worsened by the 'dumping' of difficult-to-house families. At its worst there is widespread fear of burglary and the threat (or actual) of physical violence. It is widely reported that relatively few families cause enormous amounts of physical, environmental and social damage. Fear of intimidation and victimisation for reporting crimes to authority is widespread. (Proposals to provide greater witness protection and strengthening legislation to deal with social nuisance are to be welcomed, but these should not be seen as direct answers. They need to be supported by the rebuilding of civic networks of trust and social order that can seek to lessen the causes of such disturbance. In the language of the last chapter, longer-term solutions are likely to be 'horizontal' rather than through strengthening 'vertical dependencies'.)

Energies and skills: Despite the bleakness of living conditions and the chronic lack of self-esteem that will usually accompany this, most estates will contain a variety of people with energy and skills. These need to be supported and encouraged; even meeting to address local conditions – of putting one's head above the parapet – may be risking confrontation or vandalism in the worst cases. Those who live beyond the normal boundaries of social control have a vested interest in keeping conditions the way they are.

By conducting their own audits of needs and activity, residents can make contact across neighbourhoods and start developing their own agendas for improvement. They can give support to what is already happening and begin to identify gaps.

Local knowledge and professional knowledge: In many cases the things that local people identify as, for example, health, housing and environmental improvement priorities, are not those of the professionals involved. What will seem obvious to the professional may be seen quite differently by local people. (Two brief case studies of civic entrepreneurs in Chapter 6 [pp 104-8] illustrate how such gaps can be closed.) And this is not always to do with unrealistic expectations. Particularly in areas experiencing social disruption and destabilisation, local people cannot understand why money is being spent by public bodies that they know will not produce sustainable change.

What is desperately needed in these conditions is dialogue between professionals and local people. It is not that either 'knowledge' is superior; it is likely that both are valid but not complete in themselves. As the 'Planning for Real' slogan has it – professionals should be on tap rather than on top[1]. Unfortunately, what so often happens in community consultation exercises is the opposite to any felt dialogue. Many people in the community know that consultation is a prerequisite for professionals obtaining resources. Further, they find it difficult to make sense of spending patterns that may result. They are left feeling angry and abused by the process. What may be dressed up as empowerment can have the reverse consequences. Consultation fatigue sets in.

Local capacity and agenda building: The evidence is overwhelming that where stronger community controls and social stability are developed, and where resources increasingly match locally-based agendas, then regeneration becomes sustainable. Hence there is a need for capacity and agenda building to lead the regeneration process rather than be added as an afterthought. Statutory partners need to proceed at the pace of the community and regeneration bidding and spending matched to this pace.

Community activists need support in order to extend their networks of inclusivity, involvement and activity. Voluntary and statutory bodies have their own support staff. Community groups need theirs also to help with the work of local audit and planning. Increasingly they need skills for working effectively together, negotiating with delivery agencies, funding bodies and the plethora of other potential partners and stakeholders. Confidence skills and knowledge can then increase to meet, in part, the enormous disparity in resources, know-how, and knowledge between communities and agencies. Effective community partners need access to their own technical and professional support. This is much more than 'training'. It requires support for action and learning and confidence building through action. This in turn begets growing community networks and collective learning – 'public learning'.

Mainstream spend and local partnership: A further critical factor in success is the bending of mainstream spending in local areas to address local needs. Targeted special initiatives can be effective in kick-starting renewal but it is unlikely to be sustained without the reshaping of local mainstream service delivery. But, in contrast, over-reliance on special funding may, from the agencies' perspective, serve to take the focus and pressure away from existing services. While it produces short-term quick hits, the end product may be weaker, less locally-focused services and decreased community capacity.

If special funding is available, this should be used to facilitate and add to the process of inter-agency partnership working at the front line. Additional funding can then be used to implement locally-agreed priorities. This will itself serve to reshape local mainstream delivery. Thus, as local partnerships between professions, across agencies and with communities develop, each separate element becomes part of an increasingly self-sustaining whole. This is not merely operational consultation and involvement. It is about residents becoming involved as increasingly equal partners in the strategic overview of community building with the linking of short-term needs to longer-term and wider perspectives. Sadly, this happens all too infrequently.

Power sharing and new forms of local governance:

> **"It is not good enough for local authorities and central government to make statements about how the community must be on board. They must believe what they say, they must commit to the principle of working in partnership. This is the central message of our research." (A. McGregor, 'Action on estates' video, which illustrates the main themes in Taylor, 1995)**

Partnership is not, of course, a new idea. But the new research puts the requirement on "the involvement of the main players in a *strategic* partnership which involves the residents as *equal* partners" (McArthur, 1995). In general terms, there is an enormous imbalance between residents and other partners along any dimension that can be conceived with the exception of 'local knowledge'. It is thus essential that there is a continuing search for models and structures that are capable of rebalancing this imbalance. They need to be inclusive and open, capable of including the variety of views and interests likely to be present across a neighbourhood. Such an 'umbrella' body also needs to draw in other, often excluded, groups such as youth, ethnic minorities, elderly people and disabled people

This is notoriously difficult territory. There are frequent accusations that local organisations of this type can be taken over by unrepresentative factions and entryists. Doubtless this can be a problem, but it is also a useful excuse for professionals maintaining their unitary control over resources. However, there is a relatively small, but growing, number of such umbrella bodies which have achieved legitimacy through accessibility and accountability.

Such bodies can then engage in local contracting and managing local services as well as having their own budgets and devolved staff. They can act as the sponsors for, or become successor organisations to major regeneration schemes. Above all they have to work on the basis of agreed, open, and shared agendas between all the parties involved.

District-wide partnerships: Before the new government's requirement for district-wide partnership many local authority districts have some kind of multi-agency partnership between public sector bodies, the business community and the voluntary sector. These may have been constituted for a variety of reasons, but the most significant one was to make the necessary joint applications for funding for special projects as this is likely to be a requirement of the funding bodies concerned. However, many see their work as done once funding has been acquired. From this perspective, implementation is largely a matter of putting the approved delivery plan into operation.

Comment has already been made how delivery plans frequently consist of projects, each with its own schedules, specific outputs and responsible officer. Each is usually situated within the operational hierarchy of a local authority department or other public service agency. There is therefore a very real danger that the projects become fragmented and the resulting disconnections merely follow the fault lines of the existing departmentalisation. For instance, SRB is holistic in intention by drawing together a whole series of national funding initiatives and administering it through the multi-functional regional government offices. But on the ground the activity and funding tends to become disaggregated and piecemeal, compounded by each project developing its own mechanics for consultation.

District-wide partnerships can have a very significant role in promoting sustainable regeneration but this is often little understood! They need to give direction both within and across their separate agencies to create the operational cultures and ways of working that will lead to implementation on the ground. In essence they must create the receptive conditions required for horizontal integration of service provision around emerging community agendas. This cannot be done by top-down plans, nor by *service-based* community plans.

Community and organisational learning – working with the bigger picture: There is no blueprint for tackling any of the above; each locality or neighbourhood is different with its own problems as well as community assets. Individuals and their growing networks of supporters, whether initially in the community or as front-line service deliverers, can make a significant difference. Frequently this means running against both neighbourhood and organisational cultures. Sometimes there is significant senior support but often not.

Each successful local partnership involves trial and error, although in *process* terms there are the common strands being drawn out here. Significantly, people have to learn new ways of doing things together which cross existing gaps and divides; between people in the community, between service providers and agencies and between professionals and local people. Not only is this about new skills, knowledge and perceptions, essentially it is about trust building, openness and power sharing. This happens because the diversity of people and the diversity of experience, talent and knowledge (professional and local) that they bring, start to create common sense and meaning together by building a bigger picture of the future. It is from this that individuals take their actions that can bring the bigger picture into being. The *community plan* is largely in people's heads and is shared across the closing divides. Certainly there will be a plan of paper, but it is borne out of action-based learning in a community of the whole system. The key to change is this 'public learning' based on action. It cannot be substituted by grand organisational designs and 'remote' professionally produced community plans. Such plans are not action and are unlikely to be owned by those they are supposed to be for – local people.

This can be seen as working with the bigger picture at the local level. The next question is, how can those with district-wide executive authority act to create receptive conditions to promote such change? Before looking at this there is a need to look at a further aspect of sustainable community building.

Building district-wide community networks: The evidence strongly suggests that success is more likely when the focus for regeneration has a small-area focus[2]. Residents can build more trust in what is local and personal. However, success also requires, as is evident from the need for city- (district-) wide partnerships, local development to be connected into wider networks[3]. Indeed, one of the contributing factors to the impoverishment of disadvantaged areas has been their increasing isolation from the wider systems that surround them.

Anne Power writes,

Can the need for a small-area focus and collective local provision be reconciled with the need for integration within the wider city? Cities only work small area by small area. They are made up of many parts, interacting and constantly moving. The size and shape of urban components are constantly changing. When cities are run with over-centralised systems, the strong get more, since they have better access to the larger system. That is why poor areas need to be targeted with ring-fenced and localised resources and why small area programmes are central to successful renewal. Crucially, those small, localised, intensively managed, collective programmes must happen across many areas if cities as a whole are to work and the problem is not simply to be moved around.

Many of the local solutions we found were ad hoc because of the overcomplexity of wider strategies, the high cost and long time-scale of all-embracing solutions. A fluid and reactive approach allowed new forms of problem-solving; it encouraged detailed and locally specific solutions. (Power, 1997, p 389)

This indicates the need for the development of interconnected, interactive planning processes that link neighbourhoods to districts to regions; an idea which is developed further in Chapter 6.

Further evidence and experience indicates that many of the same processes are successful in working in areas which do not, on the face of it, suffer the same levels of officially audited disadvantage as those targeted for regeneration. Capacity building and strengthening social cohesion may be a felt need in many more affluent communities as well as those that might be perceived to be deteriorating. So, there is a strong argument to say that the encouragement and support of local community-led auditing and planning around needs, strengths and emerging community agendas has intrinsic merits in any locality. It is clearly important for agencies to work laterally with localities.

But there is just as strong an argument that the localities themselves need to be able to connect and communicate with each other. Firstly, communities can learn about successes and problems in other areas and can gain confidence in what they can do and achieve. Secondly, it enables people to appreciate the diversity of situations, people and experiences, which is both directly enriching and serves to counter the fragmentation of the communal[4]. Thirdly, it helps to mitigate the divisive competitive tendencies inherent in many of the bidding processes for additional funding where communities may often feel at the whim of remote power brokers in the agencies, especially in local government. Fourthly, an arena where communities can link and meet allows for the expression of wider district needs expressed from the grass roots. This can serve as a more visible pressure and stimulus for agency and inter-agency change that focuses on the citizen in the community. Fifthly, this serves to reverse the recent trends in many areas of increasing ghettoisation of rich and poor areas alike, resulting from widening levels of inequality often linked to rising and/or feared levels of criminality.

It is this reasoning that forms the basis for the development of the C2M project in Bradford (Chapter 6, pp 112-18) and informs our ideas for the establishment of 'middle ground frameworks' in Chapters 6 and 9.

Notes

[1] 'Planning for Real' is a particular technique designed to facilitate community involvement developed by the Neighbourhood Initiatives Foundation (NIF), The Poplars, Lightmoor, Telford TF4 3QN.

[2] This is supported by much of the research quoted above. Also, according to Power, 1997, "Residents expressed more faith in personal and local than in the remote and all-embracing systems" (p 389).

[3] Power then goes on to say,

> **... the pieces of the patchwork of solutions needed to fit with all the adjacent pieces and had to be firmly joined to them on all sides, if the patchwork approach itself was to work. The argument for small local units of organisation is part of a bigger urban strategy, implying hundreds of such units, operating together. We are not describing a seamless web, but a complex, variegated, colourful pattern of many contrasting but linked parts. It is the variety, colour and movement that makes city areas attractive. (Power, 1997, p 389)**

[4] Power (1997, p 389) quotes William Wilson who "argues, almost ferociously, for forms of support that help richer, as well as poorer, neighbourhoods as a way of ensuring continuing local programmes for the poor" (Wilson, 1996).

FIVE

Change that works – sustaining organisational and whole system change

> ... organizational learning is not the same thing as individual learning, even when the individuals who learn are members of the organization. There are too many cases in which organizations know less than their members. There are even cases in which the organization cannot seem to learn what every member knows. (Argyris and Schon, 1978, p 9)

Sustaining organisational change

[This section is adapted from *Whole system development* by David Wilkinson, Margaret Attwood and Mike Pedler (1999: forthcoming) to be published by Lemos & Crane and from 'Whole system development: rethinking public service management' by David Wilkinson, published in the *International Journal of Public Sector Management*.[1]]

If we wish to tackle the obdurate 'wicked issues', to address the essential requirement to rebuild social cohesion, to place more emphasis on prevention rather than just on cure, then this has deep transformational implications for how the delivery agencies in particular define their roles in service delivery. It also has significant ramifications for how all stakeholders work together and apart. But the emphasis here will be on the public service bodies and local government in particular because their impacts are clearly so significant.

The current domination of vertical, silo-based cultures in most of the public services has been discussed in Chapter 2. The focus on improving service efficiency and effectiveness has been predominantly within these 'tower blocks' and directed around functional and 'easily counted' output measures. The guiding rationale can be described as managerialist and consumerist (see notes in Chapter 2). In general there has been a far greater requirement to seek customer satisfaction, which is of course a step in the right direction. But there are also severe limitations with this approach. For instance, it is likely that many local authorities will approach Best Value from this position and submit an increasing proportion of silo-based services to best value scrutiny. But this is unlikely to help the holistic requirement of the community agenda. Worse, it is likely to focus staff attention in entirely the wrong direction.

A community focused agenda clearly requires local integration of service professionals around community-based agendas. It is, for the most part, a radically different way of working across professional boundaries with a radically different working relationship with *service users in the community*. The focus is upon collectively understood outcomes which support the improvement of quality of life and well-being. They are future-oriented and developmental rather than quick fix; process-based, rather than recipe-driven and have a natural affinity with Local Agenda 21 (LA21). The implications for organisational and cultural change are profound, as they are for leadership, political and managerial styles.

There is the very real difficulty already alluded to earlier in the previous chapter. Public service managers frequently know and use the language of holistic and systemic change but are constrained to act within mechanistic structures and thinking styles. So the language of, say, SRB for example, at both civil service and local levels, will be redolent with the phraseology of regeneration, much of this taken from Joseph Rowntree and similar research. But it is shorn of meaning. Many have little real knowledge or understanding of the research work – a tendency accentuated by the 'not-invented-here' syndrome. It appears to be thought of as information for community workers with little implication for themselves other than the 'formal' attendance at necessary partnership meetings – feeding the (funding) beasts. Again, means are confused with ends. It is because of the widespread confusion that this causes that we have developed the Whole System Best Value matrix to help unpick the paradigmatic shift in thinking and action required to reach beyond managerialist consumerism towards an holistic community, laterally integrated leadership of public provision (see Chapter 7, pp 135-6).

So, what do we know about leading and sequencing such processes? To start with, there are some significant implications in the regeneration research work already quoted. But there is a growing interest in whole system-based approaches to change which have long historical roots in managerial theory and practices. These have mainly been developed in the private sector but also in some therapeutic practices in the caring professions. Of particular interest in this context is a variety of research about transformational change from a variety of public and private sources, including health and education[2]. Some of this is summarised in other sources[1].

Holistic research

But before illustrating some of the main messages coming out of this research, it is important to say a little more about research approaches to change. Andrew Pettigrew et al (1992) make a plea for research about change that is:

- processual   – an emphasis on action as well as structure;
- comparative   – a range of studies of local (healthcare) agencies;
- pluralistic   – describe and analyse the often competing versions of reality seen by actors in change processes;
- historical   – take into account the historical evolution of ideas and actions for change as well as constraints within which decision makers operate.

Significantly, but not surprisingly, this is itself an holistic approach. There needs to be far more research and evaluation carried out from these perspectives, especially if the community governance agenda is to make progress. Currently, it seems that too many examples of good practice take the form of case studies with little examination of the deeper contexts and processes at work. They often have too much of a 'and-in-one-leap-Jack-was-free' character about them led by leaders and/or consultants of 'heroic' status. Research methods will need to be sufficiently robust and holistic if they are to contribute to both the evaluation of innovation in support of the emerging new public service agenda and in the methods of transmitting good practice. From the perspective of this report, there will be a continuing danger that both research methods and the process of dissemination will be pressed to provide easy blueprints and 'techniques' rather than confront the often painful, personal and organisational learning that deeper level change almost always incurs.

Key messages about transformational change

The changes from which these messages were drawn was transformational because the leaders concerned recognised that organisations were faced with severe challenges. These required them to make dramatic improvements to the quality and efficiency of the goods or services involved. They recognised the need for real ownership of change, and therefore implementation of the changes, by front-line staff. Because the critical questions facing the organisation were new and required new and as yet unknown responses, there was widespread recognition for an increasing number of staff at all levels being drawn into innovation and learning while addressing the key business tasks. It meant getting beyond the traditional 'control and command' organisation and developing empowered staff working on key tasks according to knowledge, skills and potential contribution, rather than formal position or hierarchical/departmental loyalty.

Effective leadership

The studies, although drawn from very different domains including public service Britain and private sector America, and with few common research threads, are startlingly similar in their findings. They all trace a similar path to organisational renewal. But to do this strategic leadership is vital to starting, directing, supporting and monitoring this pathway.

> **Each revitalisation leader had to find a way to translate external pressures into internalised dissatisfaction with the status quo and/or excitement about a better way. Dissatisfaction is fuelled by awareness that the organisation is no longer meeting the demands of its competitive environment. Excitement can be stimulated by imagining an approach to organisation and managing that eliminates many current problems or appeals to fundamental values. (Beer et al, 1990)**

Other factors that emerge are that effective change leaders:
- Develop inclusive networks both within and beyond the boundaries of their organisations.
- Work to build open-ended and incomplete visions which are themselves inclusive of other perspectives – avoiding 'visions that blind' (an apt expression of Michael Fullan's, Dean of the Faculty of Education, University of Toronto – this was used as the title of an article in *Education Leadership*, February 1992).
- Give as much attention to processes of continual vision making as to the vision itself.

- Are able to work with others to prioritise and link change initiatives while ignoring or shelving others despite strong external top-down pressure.
- Keep a focus on the longer term and are thus able to steer around or through the turbulence of the stream of government and other external turbulence, many of which are short-term knee-jerk political responses or managerial fads (every issue is famous for 15 minutes).
- Link the priorities to dealing with locally-perceived needs and change requirements.
- Orchestrate top-down outside demands to create and focus internal attention by creating constructive tensions and energy for change where it is currently being resisted.
- Create frameworks of inclusion – often cross-departmental and agency working groups constructed on the basis of energy, skills and potential rather than formal hierarchy.
- Encourage frameworks where such groups develop integrated processes for reflection and monitoring their activity.
- Model inclusive behaviours that encourage the growing spider's web of people and activity working in similar ways.
- Work with others to develop planning processes to take invention forward; this is more likely to place the stress on planning rather than on plans themselves which are so likely to be disrupted by the turbulence of events.
- Connect this planning to, and where necessary distinguish it from, the inevitable reports, contracting and so on required by 'higher authorities' (feeding the beast) such as commissioners, regulatory bodies, OFSTED etc.
- Through all the above, create conditions where professionals and others, who frequently work in isolation – the professional silos of the health service, the individual isolation of the classroom teacher, for example – start to work with each other as learning partners; it is through this that people start to build new common sense and commonly held meaning together.
- Welcome diversity.
- Recognise that change is stressful and anxiety producing because it means letting go of old ways of doing things. In this they 'hold' both the tensions, conflicts, anxieties and excitements that are endemic in fundamental change (see Heifetz, 1994 and Heifetz and Laurie, 1997).

It is evident that when this is compared to the parallel work of community building, leadership is directed to bringing people together across the boundaries and divides that keep people apart. It is largely about working in the spaces. And it inevitably involves the open release of conflict and difference – working where the community and organisational pain is. Only so much can be dealt with and so leadership work of this kind, which requires the whole system to engage in 'adaptive work' (Heifetz, 1994), takes place over time. It requires working with widening circles of inclusivity (Wilkinson, 1997b; Pedler, forthcoming), and of using vertical authority to direct and support lateral connectivity.

Programmatic changes, in contrast, appear to offer orderly and planned change. Given the right programme, or leader, or expert consultant, it can be conducted largely risk free – or so it seems to suggest. Indeed structure and order – programmatic change in fact – can be seen as a defence against anxiety, particularly for the planners of change. Of course this is not an argument for not planning, rather that learning comes through purposeful and reflective action in dealing with difficult questions. It is important to distinguish between planning as a process and the plan itself (planning as learning, strategy as emergent: see de Geus, 1988 and Mintzberg, 1994). The plan informs action and reflection about this action informs the plan. Effective planning and strategising that is linked to the solving of real problems on the ground (rather than the more synthetic ones of isolated planners at civic headquarters) will always have this emergent property – a mix of previous intention and learning through the experience of doing.

The critical path to organisational renewal

The approach towards (and the underlying assumptions behind) the vast majority of planned change in the public services is programmatic. To be sure, many of the previous changes have involved people in high levels of adaptive learning and uncertainty but this is frequently not recognised nor used purposefully and constructively. While programmatic change will produce some silo-based change it will not be successful in producing the kinds of change required by a community focused new public service agenda. Programmatic change, its limited success and the perennial dangers of it sliding into mad management disease are discussed in Chapter 2.

In contrast to this, study of transformational change reveals the emergence of what is described elsewhere (Beer et al, 1990) as the critical path to organisational renewal. This can be described as a general manager-led (strategic leader) process that leads to business aligned implementation through the following stages:

1. Mobilising energy for change among all stakeholders in the organisation [and beyond, where appropriate] by involving them in a diagnosis of the problems blocking competitiveness.
2. Developing a business-aligned vision of how to organise and manage for 'competitiveness' [or effectiveness].
3. Fostering consensus that the new vision is 'right', competence to enact it, and cohesion to move change along.
4. Spreading revitalisation to all departments [of the organisation/business unit] in a way that avoids perception that a programme is being pushed from the top, but at the same time ensures consistency with the organisational changes already under way.
5. Consolidating changes through formal policies, systems, and structures that institutionalise revitalisation.
6. Continually monitoring and strategising in response to problems [that inevitably arise] in the revitalisation process. (Beer et al, 1990)

[Note: square brackets indicate alterations to the original text.]

At the risk of reiteration, the role of leaders is shown to be critical. It is through their strategic understanding that they are able to prioritise the strategic agenda and then use this as the focus for risk taking and innovative processes for involvement around the key business issues. Hence, as people take on these changes in responsibility and roles, they have a stake in coordinating with each other in order to achieve results because they can see how their task aligns with the bigger picture. This in turn leads to higher levels of commitment. But these new business-aligned groupings – task forces, project groups, ad hoc work teams – are tackling problems and issues that are new and that there is a desperate need to solve. They are essentially engaged in action learning – the iterative process of learning about the diagnosis of and solving real problems as well as learning about applying this new learning to the messy and complex world of real organisational life.

There is often a view that leaders need to be charismatic and perhaps aspire to hero status. This is mistaken. Effectiveness is more usually an outcome of determination, personal openness and the integrity and honesty experienced by others around them. Leaders communicate more by what they do, champion and support, than by what they say. They are able to *substantially* increase the stock of leadership across the system, generating a wide commitment to act, learn and take risks. It is the feedback from this that in turn sustains effective leaders. It is important that leaders find their own styles, and can act with a range of styles contingent upon the situation. Above all, they need to be able to live and work with paradox, dilemmas, and uncertainty – both their own and others. Courage is probably more appropriate than charisma.

It is at this stage that training, development and 'process' consultancy are likely to become important. In the language of Reg Revans[3], the founder of action learning, individuals and groups need to define questions *in their own minds* (Q) before they can fully utilise programmed knowledge and information (P) – benchmarking, visiting other workplaces, books, conferences, courses – in developing and trying out new solutions. These attempted applications together with newly emerging problems become the sources for sustaining a continuing learning process. Consultancy centring around facilitating these change and question formulation processes is likely to be extremely helpful. There is likely to emerge a self-assessed felt need by individuals and groups for training programmes, conferences, and so on that address identified knowledge and skill gaps – a requirement for 'just in time' training. There is then a thirst for knowledge, information and new skills (see Box 6).

Box 6: Reg Revans and action learning

Reg Revans is the founder of action learning, probably the most radical and innovative approach to learning and development. Sadly, much of his work has been ignored, especially its approaches to wider social, organisational and system changes. His career has been wide and extraordinarily varied. He has been, among other things, Olympic athlete (triple jump), researcher in nuclear physics at the Cavendish Laboratories, educational administrator, a developer in the newly nationalised postwar coal industry and Professor at the Manchester College of Technology from 1955.

His basic premises are that:
- There can be no learning without action, and no considered action without sober reflection.
- Without learning there can be no real change and that for both personal and organisational survival and health, learning has to be greater than, or equal to, the rate of change.
- Any person (manager) who wishes to work with change – change others – must risk changing themselves. This he called "the principle

of insufficient mandate; managers who cannot change their predisposing views of their own resistant problems during their efforts to treat those problems will never be able to make progress with them ... managers are themselves necessarily changed in the act of changing what may or first seem to be unchangeable" (Revans, 1982, pp 637-8).

- Real problems (for example, what John Stewart has called the 'wicked issues') do not have ready-made answers. They are not puzzles where the answer lies within existing 'programmes' or experts, or answers at the back of a book. Rather they are real questions which have to be explored and understood individually and collectively.
- Those who experience and share problems together – 'comrades in adversity' – should work together to seek clarification of their problems, undertake their own investigations into the wider system and work with stakeholders in the system for their improvement.

Revans developed an extensive range of action learning/research projects across a wide range of locations including industrial organisations, hospitals, mines and schools and involved staff and stakeholders at all levels. This work was developed from the 1950s to the 1970s and sadly remains largely forgotten. The best account of this work is contained in the classic collection of 50 essays, papers and articles, *The origins and growth of action learning* (1982) written between 1933 and 1981, which is sadly now out of print.

He stressed the value of workers and managers working together to solve problems and provides endless evidence for the success of this. In one extensive piece of work in the late 1960s he and field staff worked on the problems of the care of the mentally handicapped and mentally sick (as they were then designated) in the community. This involved providers across health and social services as well as 'consumers' working directly to understand the effectiveness of the then current system of care (across boundaries) and taking steps to improve it (Revans, 1982, 'Helping each other help the helpless', pp 467-92).

His work gives a clear indication of a wide range of methodologies, highly appropriate to addressing the kind of issues raised in this report and the challenges of implementing holistic government. It is perhaps symptomatic, both of the insularity of the public service establishment and the state of management and organisational development within them, that his work was largely ignored and is now almost completely forgotten.

One strand does remain; that of action learning sets for individual managers. This is a useful method of problem solving and development. But, for the most part, it has been appropriated into the 'management constituency' and action learning shorn of much of its whole system origins and approach. As such it has been rendered largely programmatic.

From this point, the workforce would develop bottom-up coaching, appraisal and development systems. Formal restructuring would often follow the informal pathways people had followed to develop new effective and high trust working practices. Again, this reverses most private and public sector approaches.

Leaders also have to work with a further dilemma; being on the one hand focused on the hard aspects of direction, business results and the necessity for change, while on the other hand realising that the new levels of commitment and competence will only come to full fruition through the development of new levels of collaboration, trust, self-managing, and genuine empowerment. This means being both driving and determined while being able to let go sufficiently for people to explore and learn the new ways of working; making the link between short-term business demands and long-term capability development.

There is a characteristic error made by managers inexperienced in spreading revitalisation.

> **They confuse insisting on a particular solution to a problem with insisting on a *process* for finding the solution. Spreading renewal requires the management of paradox. The revitalisation leader must be directive about his or her desire to see all departments engage in a process that will move them towards an emerging vision, but he or she must be non-directive about a particular way each department chooses to implement that vision. This careful balancing act is important not only to build commitment, but also to ensure that revitalisation is customised to meet the particular needs of each main area. (Beer et al, 1990, p 93)**

Assumptions about change

From these perspectives, it is now possible to distinguish more fully between the two approaches, and the basic assumptions they make about organisational change. In the business alignment approach, the focus of learning and change is upon the business task, the group and roles and responsibilities. It largely assumes that attitude change and culture change will flow from the behaviours needed to address the new agendas. The assumptions behind programmatic change processes are very different. Here the focus throughout is upon the individual and there is a tendency to assume that behaviour change follows attitude change (though not exclusively). Attempts to change culture are themselves individually focused and 'distanced' from work on business agendas or cross-boundary working experience. Learning is 'training' focused rather than 'action' focused. Also, learning is seen as individual – that is, situated in the individual – whereas in the business alignment model there is a much more public, collectivist approach where learning and meaning is both situated in the individual *and* in the group or community.

Programmatic approaches to change are also likely to assume a machine metaphor for organisational and managerial function. Here change can be anticipated and thus planned and largely detailed top-down. Only a few (the planners) have the big picture and it is assumed that the implementation will result from each person working to their appropriate script and sub-targets. It is the job of managers to coordinate and exercise detailed supervision to ensure the smooth working of their parts of the machine. While somewhat stereotyping the approach, it is clear that it provides little flexibility for lateral, cross-agency working or corresponding flexibility to local need. The main focus is upon vertical alignment and coordination of the parts; the hope is that improvement to the parts will lead to improvement of the whole. In practice, however, attempts to improve the parts more often lead to damaging and competitive suboptimism with organisational implications that echo Putnam's description (Chapter 3, pp 54-6) of the damaging effects of vertical networks on the erosion of civic society.

In contrast, 'critical path' approaches tend to assume much more organic, systems-based metaphors and thinking. This emphasises the interconnectedness of things and the requirement for widespread responsiveness and learning. People in the system need to be much more self-managing because they are working from a bigger picture that they have had a hand in creating. Top-down direction and review is essential but planning cannot replace learning and forecast the unpredictable and the currently unknowable. Business alignment/ 'critical path' approaches serve to strengthen lateral organisational and inter-organisational links, corresponding directly to Putnam's findings about the links between overlapping horizontal networks of 'weak ties' and the development of reciprocity and trust that undergird a robust civic society.

The sequencing and purposes of change interventions

Beer et al (1990) also provide a very useful insight into why the critical path process works in terms of the sequencing and purposes of intervention. Interventions are classified along two dimensions: those that focus on the individual versus the organisation as a whole, and those that focus on informal behaviour versus formal organisation design. This is illustrated in Table 1 (p 79).

Initially the critical path to organisational renewal starts typically with a leader or leaders who use their strategic understanding to create conditions of readiness and receptivity. There will need to be sufficient dissatisfaction in the system to create the potential for readiness to change. But in addition there needs to be sufficient 'slack' to allow people to express and work through this dissatisfaction to create conditions of receptivity where increasing numbers of the organisation's membership can engage in shaping the emerging vision and its implementation.

The first stages (1) of implementation are those at the organisation/ business unit level and they seek to modify informal behaviour by supporting the regrouping of roles, responsibilities and relationships around key business priorities. As people work on the real questions and problems of finding and implementing new solutions, they are likely to start to identify their own individual and team development needs (2). As this progresses, there is likely to be more widespread agreement and ownership of more formalised systems to bring together and meet these needs (3). Where this happens these systems are likely to be seen as facilitating the business of the organisation rather than being imposed distractions from doing 'real work'. Finally, formal structures, together with compensation, information and measurement systems, serve to support the new ways of working that have already come into being; the formal follows the informal as the evidence of successful implementation builds (4).

Programmatic changes are more likely to start at point (4) on the matrix and attempt to work anticlockwise back to (1). The inherent problem is the difficulty of ever breaking out of the starting ethos of formal top-down intervention (4). The difficulty is that individual and small 'in-tact' team development (2) and the development systems that are supposed to support this (3) are never owned by the majority of the organisation's membership. The likelihood is that the informal changes in roles, responsibilities and relationships that are the key to business alignment (1) have the subsumed under formal restructuring (4). This is a particular hazard in much of attempted change in the public sector.

Table 1: Sequencing organisational interventions for learning

	Level of focus	
	Organisation/business unit level	Individual or team level
Intervention seeks to modify: Informal behaviour	(1) Redefinition of roles, responsibilities and relationships around key business priorities	(2) Training Briefing Coaching/counselling Team building Management development programmes
Formal design	(4) Organisation structure Information systems Compensation systems Monitoring and measurement systems	(3) Performance appraisal Replacement and recruitment Career planning Training needs assessment

Source: Adapted from Beer et al (1990)

Working with the whole system

Given that tackling the 'wicked issues' and the improvement of quality of life are to be placed at the centre of the new public service agenda, the foregoing review of change that works suggests that:

- **Public service institutions and agencies will need to promote methods of improvement and change that seek to promote horizontal networks of collaboration, both within and between them and with the citizens and communities they serve. Conversely, they need to frustrate those vertical networks which serve to protect narrow power bases of opportunism and protection and that promote relations of patronage/clientelism. This applies as much within institutions as it does to their communities. Programmatic methodologies of change will not be capable of strengthening civic society, tackling the wicked issues, promoting cross-boundary working, and moving towards preventative government. In fact,**

they are more likely to make things worse in the name of improving them. Methods of change must be appropriate to the purpose.

- Community capacity building will be an essential starting point in many localities. The focus has to be local but connected into wider systems of governance, society, employment and so on. This is the route to building social cohesion and in the longer term, renewing the social capital, so much of which has been dissipated through social, economic and market fragmentation.

- Capacity building can only be done through support systems that enable local people to do this themselves. Putting in task forces, for example, is not capacity building; at best it can support capacity building, at worst it can interrupt what is already there.

- Local partnerships need to be formed between multi-agency front-line partners and the community. These can be the seed beds for many new forms of community governance and service delivery arrangements. Any special monies need to be used as a means to create these new conditions.

- Rebalancing the power relationship between people in communities and those with resources – public service agencies and wider – is of fundamental importance to long-term sustainability.

- Strategic leaders, particularly at the district level – along with other significant stakeholders – will need to give strong leadership and direction both individually and collectively – to create organisational change conditions to move in these directions. This will mean working with change processes of holistic development with which many have little experience. The agenda simply cannot be implemented through the pursuit of programmatic change.

- Change leaders will need to avoid endless 'official' strategies for each aspect of the change agendas as well as obligations, statutory and otherwise, that already exist. They need to promote integrated strategies of social change crafted to local conditions, needs and context. Strategies need therefore to be rather more about the 'how' of change rather than the 'what'.

- Community plans, for which there is likely to be at least an administrative requirement in the future, need to be a product of genuine local partnership and agenda setting, not a statement of the professional view. And they will have to be 'local' enough to create trust and meaning in communities and neighbourhoods.

This means that effective change leadership means seeing and working with the whole system – agencies as well as communities. One part cannot be altered without changes elsewhere. And the whole is so complex that it cannot be planned top-down. Change will need to be organic, at times experiential, and above all action-oriented. It will also take time. The current state of things has taken many years to evolve to its present condition. It is naive to think that radical change of the kind required can happen overnight. For policy makers, this represents something of a paradox: on the one hand, the need to provide sufficient external stimulus to promote change (ie short-term requirement to change) while on the other, giving sufficient support to public service bodies to tackle transformational changes required (ie the long-term development of organisational capacity). Change needs both shock – a perturbation – and support.

Recent research findings on developing the system of local governance

Over the past four years, the Economic and Social Research Council (ESRC) has sponsored a major programme of research on this topic under the directorship of Professor Gerry Stoker of Strathclyde University. The findings have been summarised in four important articles in the *Local Government Chronicle* by Declan Hall at Inlogov, University of Birmingham. He has charted four parallel themes that emerge from the work:

- the need for much stronger, more active citizen involvement and a move beyond narrow definitions of consumerism;
- the importance of partnerships and networks in local policy formulation and policy making;
- how politicians and officers can build effective community leadership in a more fragmented local governance system;
- the importance of processes and outcomes in managing change.

The main findings present a picture which suggests fundamental changes are beginning to take place in local government and local governance in response to external pressures for change. There are many encouraging signs which resonate with the themes being developed in this report, and which demonstrate learning on the ground in an attempt to deal with the piecemeal and episodic nature of many of the external reforms. It both shows what is being done as well as some of the constraints and the size of the task ahead. The research is also significant because it draws links between citizens, communities, services, structures and governance – the parts and the whole.

There is abundant evidence about what works to promote the implementation of holistic, preventative government. What is presented here has particular relevance to our own current levels of knowledge and experience. Despite the optimism inherent in Declan Hall's interpretation of the ESRC's sponsored research, much useful innovation still has too much of the character of swimming against the mainstream of old mind-sets and cultures. What is urgently required are more coherent structures, processes, frameworks and supports that promote this good practice on the ground. In particular policy formulation *and implementation* must surely take more account of the research evidence available. Above all, they must promote holistic, action learning and systemic-based approaches to leading change and implementation. At the same time they need to avoid the simplistic top-down programmatic approaches that have been so much in vogue, especially private sector hand-me-downs often well past their sell-by dates. But that does not mean not looking outside for good ideas.

A model for change

Developing models, metaphors and mind maps for thinking about the complex processes of change will be particularly important. Figure 1 represents a very simple model for representing the key interlinked dimensions for working with the whole district-wide system (Wilkinson, 1997b).

Figure 1: The key interlinked dimensions for the whole district-wide system

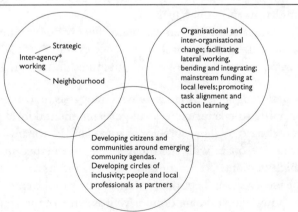

Strategic
Inter-agency*
working
Neighbourhood

Organisational and inter-organisational change; facilitating lateral working, bending and integrating; mainstream funding at local levels; promoting task alignment and action learning

Developing citizens and communities around emerging community agendas. Developing circles of inclusivity; people and local professionals as partners

* This refers to all types of organisations/agencies with a stake in the system, including individual local authority departments.

The critical starting point is with the development of an increasingly shared local agenda for change that itself emerges from a commonly held view of what a better community would be like. This will often be as much about improving the social infrastructure as with the physical infrastructure. Local agendas at the neighbourhood level are likely to be the outcome of a variety of preceding activities that involve locally-based social audits and capacity building as well as the possibility of social and civic entrepreneuralism (see Chapter 6).

We know that a crucial element in sustaining regeneration and quality of life improvement lies in how mainstream spending is reconfigured around these community agendas. Dick Atkinson, in a forthcoming Demos publication, illustrates what poor value is obtained in many localities from the way much of this is currently spent. The reasons for this are inherent in our own analysis so far. Sadly, much regeneration effort over the past 25 years has hidden this by parachuting in what has effectively been largely substitute money. Atkinson calls for the disassembly of "the budgets and inputs of mainstream departments" and their re-assembly "at the level of each neighbourhood in order to tackle its problems and meet locally agreed outputs and targets". This process, it should be pointed out, is being developed by Walsall Council with the direct involvement of key partner agencies. Thus, to implement this change model, there will have to be a radical transformation of the ways in which public services are configured, led and organised. And the focus for this must be community agendas, not the tick box requirements of civic headquarters and government departments and agencies.

Finally, partnership resulting in genuine multi-agency working is both the driving force and the cement required to produce the necessary changes. But we know that the key place where this matters is at the front line, between professionals, delivery agencies in the localities and local people themselves. Seen in this light, district/county-wide inter-agency partnerships around for example, health action, local government renewal, regeneration, and crime and disorder, are strategic and *back-line*. They should be there to create the conditions for the necessary front-line neighbourhood-based partnerships. And it is at this level where the bulk of involvement and dialogue should be 'merged' to reflect the indivisible nature of local problems and their causes *so that the causes can be jointly tackled*.

Currently, much of the frenetic partnership activity that is taking place at the district level is being pursued as though that in itself is the partnership that is required. As such, it will be incapable of producing the changes that are required, becoming the latest example of all hat and no cattle.

The New Deal for Communities programme set out in the Social Exclusion Unit's report, *Bringing Britain together: A national strategy for neighbourhood renewal* (1998) clearly indicates that some lessons from the past have been learned. In his introduction to the report, the Prime Minister, Tony Blair, writes:

> **It pulls no punches. It shows that for too long governments have simply ignored the needs of many communities. When they have acted the policies haven't worked. Too much has been spent on picking up the pieces, rather than building successful communities or preventing problems from arising in the first place. Often huge sums have been spent on repairing buildings and giving estates a new coat of paint, but without matching investment in skills, education and opportunities for the people who live there.**
>
> **Too much has been imposed from above, when experience shows that success depends on communities themselves having the power and taking the responsibility to make things better. And although there are good examples of rundown neighbourhoods turning themselves around, the lessons haven't been learned properly.**

In describing a new national strategy for poor neighbourhoods, the report says that "a huge effort" will be required "to re-think policies that have failed" (Social Exclusion Unit, 1998, p 10).

It will mean learning the lessons of the past and:
- investing in people, not just buildings;
- involving communities, not parachuting in solutions;
- developing integrated approaches with clear leadership;
- ensuring mainstream policies really work for the poorest neighbourhoods;
- making a long-term commitment with sustained political priority (Social Exclusion Unit, 1998, p 10).

New Deal for Communities places much greater emphasis of involving communities from the start and wanting them fully involved in developing bids for larger amounts of extra funding, recommendations that are made at the end of this report. This is heartening. However, the speed with which a single neighbourhood has to be decided in each of the 17 selected local authorities, means that the decisions will inevitably take place in 'top-down' committee rooms, with virtually no reference to the existing local capacity to work in this way. Further, without a clear statement of how local mainstream provision will be disassembled and reconfigured around the chosen neighbourhoods, it is likely that structural inertia of the status quo will remain largely untouched. The lure (pollution) of large amounts of extra funding – up to £45m – will re-stimulate the worst features of the institutional approach to SRB during the critical setting up, or entry, stages. This may be exacerbated by the nervous desire of civil servants and Regional Development Agencies for immediate, misleading and simplest outputs – which will of course be called outcomes because that is now the current language to use.

It is sincerely hoped that such forebodings are misplaced. But the early worry is that despite the lessons apparently learned, there may be not enough emphasis of the fundamental need to create the institutional changes required to deliver New Deal.

The main findings of the ESRC's research on developing the system of local governance

1. The need for much stronger citizen involvement

"There are four main lessons in developing citizenship and participation strategies. First, the concept of citizenship needs to go beyond narrow definitions based on consumerism to a more active concept based on accountability, participation and empowerment. Second, a more active concept of citizenship can be developed through strategies. Third, some of the main ways to empower citizens is through concentrating on a small area, backed up by council support through a balance in bottom-up strategies. Fourth, there are difficulties in developing participation and partnership strategies because of the nature of many funding mechanisms.

One study by John Boynon found that an instrumentalist and negative effect on community involvement was apparent in local crime prevention strategies. It highlighted the uneven, episodic project-centred character of partnership-based crime prevention and community safety initiatives. Accountability of the projects to local communities was found to be weak and there was little active participation by residents" (Hall, 1997a, p 15).

2. The importance of partnerships and networks in local policy formulation and policy making

"There are five main lessons here. First, there is no one template for partnerships, they need to be flexible and varied and the form a partnership of network takes depends on the task in hand.

Second, partnerships are particularly suited for economic development purposes. Third, partnerships can also be used to promote the community leadership capacity of local government.

Fourth, partnerships are two-edged swords in relation to democratic practice – they do raise issues of accountability in relation to councillors' roles but they can also be more inclusive by including a wide range of stakeholders in the policy making and service delivery process.

Fifth, networking and interpersonal skills become more important for managers of partnerships. It is these lessons local authorities need to bear in mind when they are developing and undertaking a partnership and network strategy. [Significantly the report adds,] Politicians and managers involved in the operation of partnerships and networks need a level of skills which is wider and more complex than might be needed in a more bureaucratic organisation" (Hall, 1997b, pp 16-17).

3. How politicians and officers can build effective community leadership in a more fragmented local governance

"There are five main lessons. First, the new politics of local governance presents new opportunities for councillors to develop community leadership roles. Second, councillors need to develop political networks outside traditional party structures to cultivate community leadership. Third, the new politics of local governance can present opportunities for previously excluded groups to be included in the political process via sympathetic managers. Fourth, leading councillors need to place themselves at the heart of partnerships which can increase their community leadership capacity. Fifth, councillors can best help define their community leadership roles through neighbourhood-based participation programmes" (Hall, 1997c, p 19).

There were also some significant findings about the links between locally-based decision-making processes and wider community governance roles for both officials and politicians.

"A survey by Bill Miller of Glasgow University found a lot of suspicion among the general public towards non-elected bodies in local decision making in favour of more traditional structures. Yet alongside this support for traditional elected council structures, another study of community-based housing organisations in Glasgow by David Clapham of the Cardiff

University found even more support among residents for their own community associations, even though one-third never attended meetings. Residents trusted their own associations more than central or local government. Moreover, the research showed that CBHCs also acted as a focus for local people, helping to create and sustain a sense of community and prompting a sense of ownership and control over the local area.

This gives local politicians a base upon which to develop community-based local governance and act as the focal point for community aspirations. Officials and politicians have to be more proactive in developing high-profile community governance roles, and there is a deep reservoir of public support for them to do so. A new government, committed to revitalising local communities, gives groups on local councils of all political persuasions the opportunities to lead that process" (Hall,1997c, p 19).

4. **The importance of processes and outcomes in managing change**

"The findings here illustrate that external pressures have been forcing local government to change its shape and style and 'highlighted the importance of developing new politics alongside the new management in local governance'" (Hall, 1997d, p 12).

"'Old' approaches – such as centralism, professionalism and departmentalism – also remained highly influential. The particular mix of management methods adopted by different bodies related to their political preferences, their 'organisational politics' – in terms of the role of key individuals and lead departments – and the needs and culture of their localities. The character of local government management is changing rapidly and profoundly from a system based on integrated bureaucratic and professional hierarchies to a much more diversified system. Councils are increasingly made up of a collection of different units of varying degrees of autonomy – separate purchaser and provider units, devolved budget centres, localised service outlets, arm's-length trusts and trading organisations, and so on.

Several projects studied the growing importance of networking or partnership as a means of managing change and working across organisational boundaries. Networking was seen as a potential middle way between competitive markets and hierarchical bureaucracies. Networking is, ideally, characterised by cooperation for mutual benefit, based on relations of loyalty, trust, reciprocity and interdependence. The research projects demonstrated that networks arose for a variety of reasons:

to secure funding, to address 'wicked issues', to meet statutory requirements, to overcome fragmentation in service delivery or policy making, and to facilitate learning and good practice.

Management of change in local government brings with it a wider range of relationships with the public. The public continues to be involved in local governance in the traditional roles of elector, protester and service user, but there are new opportunities through appointment to governing boards and partnership bodies and through involvement in organised user groups and consultation exercises. The research projects studied new forms of public involvement in a range of policy areas and reveal a mixed picture. While the range and volume of participation opportunities have increased, questions remain about who it is that participates and to what effect" (Hall, 1997d, p 12).

Notes

[1] Wilkinson et al (1999: forthcoming). There is a chapter entitled 'The whole system curriculum'. Also, see Wilkinson, 1997a; Wilkinson and Pedler, 1996; Wilkinson and Pedler in Garratt, 1995, pp 187-204. The best recent survey and summary of public service change in the UK which recognises at least some of this wider literature is Ferlie et al, 1996.

[2] Perhaps the most interesting and insightful history of these ideas is contained in Weisbord, 1987. The application of this thinking led to the specific development of a range of whole or large-scale intervention methodology. Weisbord, 1992 is the best introduction of the underlying principles of these designs although narrowly applied in this instance. These embrace a range of informing ideas including Weisbord (1987) above, as well as socio-technical systems thinking, psycho-therapeutic approaches to the study of group behaviour, self-regulating systems, ecological systems and behaviour, action learning and the more recent interest in the application of systems thinking in discussing learning organisations. These sources are summarised in Wilkinson and Pedler, 1996. There is also a range of empirically grounded research which describe in both process and outcome terms paths to successful organisational renewal and strategic change. In a variety of ways, and from very different contexts, they illustrate how successful leaders have fashioned leadership strategies that have stressed involvement, inclusion, valuing diversity and emphasised individual and collective learning through action, risk-taking and reflection. Key texts are Beer et al, 1990; Heckscher, 1995; Fullan, 1991; Hopkins et al, 1994; Pettigrew et al, 1992; Pascale, 1990; Dixon, 1994; Hampden-Turner and Trompenaars, 1993; Womack et al, 1990. There are very rich and

promising developments in the areas of leadership, influencing and 'meaning-making' in communities of practice. Heifetz (1994) describes the work of leaders as providing 'holding environments' while organisations and their memberships make necessary – and often painful – adaptive changes. Drath and Palus (1994) make the case for looking at leadership from a meaning-making perspective where leaders seek to engage with 'their communities' in the most productive way in order to achieve the co-creation of common meaning, that is, shared cultures and cultures that can talk to each other in pluralistic organisations. See Heifetz, 1994; Heifetz and Laurie, 1997; Drath and Palus, 1994. In a similar vein, there has been a pronounced shift from strategic planning to strategic thinking and learning. This recognises that so much that passes as strategic plans are little more than 'the view through the rear mirror' and are frequently ignored anyway. The newer perspectives talk of strategic intent, strategy as emergent and of planning as learning. See Mintzberg, 1994; Garratt, 1995; de Geus, 1988; 1997; Hamel and Prahalad, 1989; 1994.

[3] Professor Reg Revans is the 'father' of action learning. A collection of 50 articles appears in *The origins and growth of action learning* (1982), Chartwell-Bratt, Bromley, UK, written between 1933 and 1981 (sadly now out of print). For a brief introduction to action learning, see Pedler, 1996; also Revans, 1998.

SIX

Developing the middle ground: where bottom-up meets top-down (a third way for local governance?)

Only connect.... (Forster, 1910)

Public management currently lacks a public. Users have to be rebuilt into a public with a communal feeling and communal outlook. There has to be a method for doing this. (Corrigan and Joyce, 1997, p 431)

Social cohesion: strengthening or weakening?

It is quite possible to paint a picture of weakening social cohesion and the consequent deterioration of civic society and in some parts – the worst estates for example – its collapse. From this perspective, the key causes are widening inequalities, the continuing rise of economic and social individualism, weakening family structures, marriage breakdown, labour market fluidity and geographic mobility driven particularly by Anglo-American responses to globalisation. This has been an issue of increasing concern for a number of writers and commentators (Donnison, Gray, Willets; also 'The report on wealth creation and social cohesion in a free society' by the Commission on Wealth Creation and Social Cohesion set up by the Rt Hon Paddy Ashdown MP, leader of the Liberal Democrats). It is evident from the ground covered so far that these are very real concerns and underlie some of our most intractable social problems. This seems to be happening in a world where perhaps a majority are increasingly money rich and time poor while a substantial number of others are money poor and time rich[1].

But at the same time, it is also possible to write another story. Over recent years it appears that there has been an upsurge in community-based, bottom-up initiatives. Much of this has happened despite local government and public service organisations rather than because of them. It has also taken place against a background of social fragmentation. Yet voluntary activity is alive and well. Membership of voluntary organisations steadily increases, while over the long term, that of political parties falls[2].

Geoff Mulgan and Charles Landry, for instance, describe the enormous range of clubs, self-help, mutual help, voluntary activity and associated organisations.

> **If you explore any city, town or neighbourhood in Britain, you soon find an extraordinary undergrowth of voluntary action. Amateurs, enthusiasts and the committed join together in self-help groups, clubs, associations and federations, in a myriad of activities stretching from health, social welfare, leisure, recreation, education, to community development and conservation. (Mulgan and Landry, 1995, p 14)**

The following pages offer some glimpses of the high range of bottom-up activity of this type.

The expanding voluntary sector: 'a pulsating generator of innovative practice'

The latest report from the RSA's Redefining Work project (1998) charts the rapid growth of employment in this sector by 53.4% between 1993 and 1997 when it employed 516,000 people. Far from a stereotype of being backward and inefficient, it is described as being innovative, well-managed and flexible. They promote flexible working practices, are socially inclusive, create highly motivating work cultures, and perhaps particularly significantly, have developed 'spiral' rather than 'linear' career paths. Box 7 contains Meta Zimmock's summary of the report (1998).

Box 7: Meta Zimmock reveals evidence that debunks the stereotype of a backwater sector

When the RSA decided to explore the impact of changes in the nature and patterns of work in the voluntary sector it hardly suspected its findings would prove so startling.

According to the stereotype, the voluntary sector is small, inefficient, run by managerialist wannabes, and staffed by do-gooders and refugees from the 'real' world of work.

According to the RSA's revisionist view it is none of these things. It is a middling (and growing) part of the socio-economic fabric, run successfully by committed managers, and staffed by flexible, highly qualified and satisfied workers.

In short, according to the RSA's latest Redefining Work report, launched yesterday, the voluntary sector is not a backwater but a pulsating generator of innovative practices which leave it well-placed – perhaps better placed than other sectors – to function in the new world of work.

The report, which assembled data from a variety of sources and commissioned the extraction of new data from the 1993/97 Labour Force Survey, shows that the voluntary sector is expanding. There were 516,000 workers in Britain in 1997 and numbers increased by 53 per cent between 1993 and 1997. It is also more socially inclusive and more skilled than the whole workforce. Two-thirds of workers are women (compared with around 45 per cent of the whole workforce, and 3 per cent of all women workers are employed in the voluntary sector (compared with only 1 per cent of men). On average, workers in the voluntary sector are older – they join later and leave later – than the whole workforce, and there are large clusters of women aged 35-44 and men aged 45-54. A greater proportion (5 per cent) of workers are members of ethnic minorities than in the whole workforce, although the gap is narrowing. Twenty-seven per cent of workers have university degrees (compared with 15 in the whole workforce).

Voluntary-sector workers have greater than average opportunities for changing jobs and engaging in all forms of flexible working – temporary, fixed-term and part-time work, self-employment and shiftwork. Thirty-six per cent of workers work part-time (compared with 25 per cent of the whole workforce).

They are not primarily motivated by material rewards. Workers trade lower pay, up to 30 per cent less than in other sectors, for higher levels of non-material rewards such as job satisfaction and convenience - the work can often be integrated with the rest of their lives. They are passionate in their defence of their 'culture', whether it be the purity of their missions or the right to 'dress like a dog's dinner'.

The voluntary sector's workforce has developed an alternative form of career to the 'linear' norm. Rather, it is a 'spiral' career –

> moving around, not necessarily upwards, in different lines of work in small and open organisations to create the optimum environment for personal development.
>
> In a world where there may not be enough paid employment for all who want it and where survival may depend on flexibility, the voluntary sector has much to offer – an inclusive workforce, attainable goals, and a career structure which permits balance between work, family responsibilities, education, leisure and service to the community." (*The Guardian*, 10 June 1998)

The rise of the social entrepreneur

Charles Leadbeater (1997) has described this in a Demos publication under this title. Social entrepreneurs are described as follows:

- **Their output is social: they promote health, welfare and well-being.**
- **Their core assets are forms of social capital – relationships, networks, trust and co-operation – which give them access to physical and financial capital.**
- **The organisations they found are social, in the sense that they are not owned by shareholders and do not pursue profit as their main objective. These organisations are social also in the sense that they are part of civil society, rather than the state. Indeed they are innovative often because they are at odds with the central and local state.**
- **Social entrepreneurs are often community entrepreneurs, attempting to regenerate the locality, estate or neighbourhood in which they are based. However not all social entrepreneurs are based in geographically defined communities. Many serve wider constituencies. (Leadbeater, 1997, p 19)**

They share many of the characteristics which typify entrepreneurs in all walks of life.

- **They excel at spotting unmet needs and mobilise under-utilised resources to meet these needs.**
- **They are driven and determined, ambitious and charismatic. Social entrepreneurs are driven by a mission, rather than by the pursuit of profit or shareholder value.**
- **In the private sector it is quite possible to be a successful**

entrepreneur without being at all innovative. In the social sector it is far more likely that an entrepreneur will also be an innovator. [They] are entrepreneurial because they are innovative: they develop new services and organisations. (Leadbeater, 1997, pp 19-20)

The emergence of social entrepreneurs represents an important source of innovation. They fill the gaps between disadvantaged people, ailing welfare systems, and state-provided services constructed around the conditions of a past era. It is difficult to estimate how many people there are acting, at least in part, to fill these gaps. Many are unknown outside their local contexts. Undoubtedly their number is set to grow and there is a growing recognition of the significance of their roles.

The Community Action Network (CAN) has been established as an information network for the development, support and promotion of social entrepreneurs. It aims to serve as a central, well-publicised and independent resource to those operating – or seeking to operate – in this sector (Adele Blakeborough, Community Action Network, Panton House, 22-27 Haymarket, London SW2Y 4EN). CAN is also linked to the 2000 x 2000 project which seeks to establish around 2,000 social entrepreneurs across the UK early in the new millennium.

Community economic action

There is a growing range of schemes which seek to develop sustainable alternatives to gaps left in local economies resulting from market globalisation. 'Community works! A guide to community economic action', published by the New Economics Foundation, outlines 34 types of initiatives under the generic classifications of trade, money, food, energy, housing, land, transport and lifestyle. The most numerous initiatives include:

- 275 community enterprises in England and Wales and a further 170 in Scotland, the latter supporting 3,300 jobs and training places with a collective turnover of approximately £18m. Community enterprises have social aims and are run and owned by local people. There are three types: community businesses, community cooperatives and development trusts.
- Over 400 LETS (Local Exchange Trading Schemes or Systems), varying in size from a few dozen in new starts to over 700 members.

- 520 Credit Unions throughout the UK with 80,000 members and assets of £30m. This has grown from 50 ten years ago.
- 35,000 members of Food Box Schemes directly connecting food consumers to organic producers and cutting out the middle men.
- Over 500 Community Recycling Schemes. Practical action involved people in their local environments. Community groups may benefit financially and there are potential job opportunities.
- Over 50 Community Composting Schemes.
- 150 Development Trusts that are community-led enterprises with social objectives and are actively engaged in the economic, environmental and social regeneration of an area. The Coin Street Complex on the South Bank of the Thames in London is a particularly high profile example of a development run by local people rather than a property company or big developer. It features a thriving mix of restaurants, galleries, small shops and social housing around the refurbished OXO tower. The commercial profits are used to provide social housing at affordable rents for people earning below national average wages. The Development Trust Association is lobbying the government to exert pressure on banks and City financiers to enter partnerships with these trusts (see Hugill, 1998).
- 2,500 Community Transport Schemes.

This is just the tip of an iceberg of community-oriented endeavour, the outcome of the activities of numerous social activists and entrepreneurs. Alongside this there are many others who have promoted the cause of ecological sustainable local systems, organised forums, search conferences, advocated good practice and lobbied public and private organisations for improvement.

Some of the above will have been supported by public sector bodies through particular projects and initiatives. For example, Gloucestershire County Council largely contracted out of the Local Agenda 21 participation process to an established series of groups. Its vision 21 was developed in this way to gain as much ownership as possible across a broad range of groups and communities (Hall, 1997a). In many other cases, individual officers and councillors will be advocates and supporters. But for the most part, this type of activity, as with much of the rest described in this chapter, is cut from the mainstream of political and professional activity.

Broad-based organising

This a process that seeks to counter the deficit in civil society[1]. It is a "method of bringing people together from local communities across a city or region to campaign effectively on issues of common concern, to bring about change and to advance the interests of ordinary people, especially the poor and the powerless" (Foundation for Civil Society). It aims to build trust and shared values across diverse sections in society and to campaign on specific issues of common concern. It aims to influence and challenge policy makers on issues like crime, public services and the environment through the "disciplined, persistent action of coalitions of organised citizens" (Foundation for Civil Society).

Broad-based organised communities are now active in Bristol, Liverpool, Sheffield, North Wales, the Black Country and East London (Foundation for Civil Society).

Faith groups and voluntary activity

Faith groups have a particular significance in many inner city and deprived areas. They may represent one of the few surviving networks of social contact and voluntary activity. For instance, the work of Andrew Mawson at the Bromley-by-Bow Centre in London has been well chronicled by Charles Leadbeater's work on social entrepreneurs (1997, pp 37-46). There are many faith workers who give essential support to regeneration projects.

Similarly Faith in the City groups have provided significant arenas for meeting to support such essential activity. For instance, the group in Bradford created the opportunities for what has eventually become the C2M project which is reported later in this chapter.

Community Service Volunteers (CSV)

CSV exists to promote volunteering and match volunteers to community needs. The 1996/97 annual review reports a total of 156,490 volunteers providing 5,894,657 volunteer hours. Their activities include:

- The Volunteer Programme which welcomes all young people (no one is ever rejected) to give 4-12 months service away from home during which they are provided with accommodation, food and £23 per week pocket money. Young offenders, young people leaving care and people with disabilities are particularly welcomed.
- CSV Education for Citizenship mobilises undergraduates to tutor

in schools, as well as promoting community involvement related to the curriculum.

- CSV's Retired and Senior Volunteer Programme involves over 5,000 people aged 50 plus, tutoring in schools, working with 100 GP practices to give support to patients and a range of other activities chosen by the volunteers working in groups, particularly on social housing estates.
- CSV Media works with over 100 radio and television stations nationwide to promote volunteering and train unemployed people for careers in the media.
- CSV Training and Enterprise trains some 5,000 people, mainly young people, in broadly caring skills, personal care, administration, bricklaying and carpentry. This too has a non-rejection policy.
- CSV Environment works on social housing estates and with schools to engage people in improving their own environment.
- CSV Innovations provide allies for children in care and mobilise employees to work in the community with schools, on team tasks and wherever their skills and energy may be welcome (taken from information provided by CSV, 237 Pentonville Road, London N1 9NJ, Tel 0171 278 6601).

Carers and health-based self-help groups

There are about 5.7 million adults in Britain who have unpaid or informal caring responsibilities for a sick, disabled or elderly person. This is a vast, if scarce resource, of mutual aid, largely hidden and taken for granted. It may have fallen by as much as a million people since 1990, which may indicate a long-term decline in caring, particularly by relatives. A report, published by the Carers National Association, found that as many as half suffered from isolation and emotional and physical stress (1998).

It also reported that many were critical of support they received from healthcare professionals in the NHS, particularly in relation to hospital discharge and care support. However, many others reported satisfaction with the supportive help they had received from NHS staff, GPs being a particular source of information and help.

There has also been a significant rise in the number of health-based self-help groups, in part at least, the result of the needs of carers as well as of those with specific illnesses and disabilities like diabetes, strokes, cancers, Alzheimer's, Aids, drug addictions, and communities of health concerns such as women's health groups, ethnic minority groups and so on. Not only do these offer advice, counselling and emotional support, they act as a campaigning group on behalf of their membership, in part 'in revolt' against professional services as well as in negotiation with them. Some become national campaigning organisations. Mulgan and Landry write,

> **All of these different types of organisation share some features, above all a rejection of the dominant approaches to defining and resolving problems of the professions. For the professional approach to problem-solving favours structures that are formal rather than informal, decision making that is hierarchical rather than participative, language that is often jargonistic rather than everyday. Moreover the professional public bodies tend to provide services rather than support or information, are paid for rather than relying on voluntary labour, and base their knowledge on science and training rather than direct experience.**
>
> **Mutual help organisations by contrast value experience, flat structures and participation. In this respect their central principles are little different from their equivalents a century or more ago. (Mulgan and Landry, 1995, p 45)**

This provides an excellent description of the ground to be negotiated between the traditions of silo-based professionalism, managerialism and institutionalised resource power and the world of civic organisation and mutual self-help. This brings us back to key issues raised in the last chapter about the reconciliation of vertical networks of (professionally-based) hierarchy with the horizontal networks required for effective inter-agency working and creating and supporting voluntary networks and organisations that will both promote a flourishing civic society and support people's quality of life. And in the case of carers, this has particular significance particularly in the context of an ageing society. A decline in the amount of care and in the organisation of mutual self-help has enormous resource implications for the formal professional systems.

The family in decline?

It seems to be commonly accepted that family life has been in continuing decline, especially since the 1960s, marriage and family breakdown and geographical mobility being seen as the main causes. But it may be that the picture is not as gloomy as is so frequently painted. It may be, for instance, that the number of carers is falling currently, but at 5.7 million it represents an enormous resource and this is in most cases within the family. It is vital that our welfare organisations support them in ways that are sympathetic to the needs and *felt experiences* of the carers.

Further, Young and Lemos' *The communities we have lost and can regain* chart a good deal of evidence over the last 20 years that indicates that the 'virtual' family – the three-generational family, "is 'in quite a healthy state'" (Young and Lemos, 1997, pp 42-4). This provides the context for the 'lateral family' and provides considerable support for the vicissitudes of the lateral family. Indeed they help strengthen the vertical family because of the needs of child and other care and support.

These factors are a useful reminder in the face of the seemingly accepted wisdom that the family is in terminal decline. This point is made, not in defence of any particular model of family; rather to point out the enormous amount of mutual aid and support that still does take place between kith and kin.

Community capacity building and the emergence of good practice

A good deal has already been said about this in Chapter 4. It is summarised here because it is a further glimpse into what has already been achieved in local communities and the potential it holds for the future. The evidence also demonstrates its central role in any successful regeneration. But it remains an elusive idea for the dominant political and managerial mind-sets of the current era. These tend to be fixated around tough action and quick fix solutions and hard measures of targets and outcomes. Capacity building, on the other hand, is to do with developing, leading and facilitating processes between people. This is, of course, as applicable in broad terms to communities *and* organisations and the links between them. The focus is also long term – as it has to be to reverse the forces of disintegration of the last 30 years. But this is difficult for the political (irrespective of party) and managerial macho types who have become so dominant in recent years. Talk of community, process, soft outcomes, and long time scales frequently produce anguished talk of all that bad old days 'touchy-feely soft stuff'. This is sad, because it is in the gaps between people – in communities *and* organisations – where the pain is. Those who work 'in the gaps' know there is no avoidance; there is little that is soft here. In the short term, it is the sticking with the numbers of the easily countable, setting other people targets, going for the quick fix and moving on every three years before the long-term effects are seen, that is the easy option. This, together with a civic centre office and committee culture, serve to maintain a strong emotional detachment from the content of the work and the pain in many communities. Of course politicians, national and local, have to be seen to achieve short-term goals, but it would make a great difference if they and their advisers could achieve these in such a way that these did not so prejudice the long term. Any moves towards the alleviation of the wicked issues and towards holistic, preventative government, will require a balancing of such short necessities and long-term political goals.

There is a growing literature of research and practice in this field. The following provides the range of core ideas that underpin the proposals in this report.

- The research funded by the Joseph Rowntree Foundation and similar. This has already been covered in Chapter 4.
- The development of good practice guides about how to tackle community building. The work of the Community Development Foundation is especially valuable and *Building community strengths: A resource book on capacity building* by Steve Skinner is particularly useful[2].
- The New Economics Foundation has been another source of developing theory and practice in the areas of community and social indications and audit and the development and promulgation of a whole range of participative activity (New Economics Foundation [NEF], 1st Floor Vine Court, 112-166 Whitechapel Road, London E1 1JE, Tel 0171 377 5696). Their indicators show that the quality of life in Britain may have declined over the last 20 years even while GDP has nearly doubled.
- Dick Atkinson in *The common sense of community* (1994) provides a practical vision for revitalising local communities rooted in his own experience developing St Paul's community education and development agency in Balsall Heath, Birmingham. The approach takes full advantage of the previous government's policy to create self-governing (GMS) schools, promote housing associations and so on. It builds the lateral connections between clusters of local self-governing institutions and voluntary organisations working together to foster self-reliant citizens and communities. This is the means to enhancing people's sense of neighbourhood.
- In his study of crime, community and prevention, Jon Bright (1997) develops the holistic multi-agency case for shifting the emphasis of policy to prevention. It provides both an analysis of the issues and

practical ways forward which resonate with so many of the issues raised here. Prevention cannot be the sole responsibility of any one agency. The police may have a particular role, but the causes of criminality are complex. Progress depends upon a multi-agency approach that focuses on joint understanding of the problems, issues and causes. Essentially it is about working between the gaps of existing services and will cover:

 ▸ pre-school education
 ▸ parenting programmes
 ▸ youth and mentoring initiatives
 ▸ improved school attendance and performance
 ▸ better design and security of housing
 ▸ increased local community involvement.

Jon Bright also has some salient reminders about the downside of so many partnerships. There are already about 250 crime prevention partnerships and soon there will be one to cover every local authority area. Giving reasons why so many do not always achieve what is expected of them, he writes:

> **First, the partnership is seen as an end in itself rather than a means to an end. Second, there is confusion about the role of the multi-agency group on the one hand and the individual agencies on the other. Third, partnerships fail to implement a focused programme of work. Fourth, they do not address the whole problem. Finally, they fail to achieve durability. (Bright, 1997, p 82)**

To illustrate the point, he provides an example:

> **A multi-agency initiative to tackle crime problems on a housing estate may not succeed or will take much longer to work if the housing department does not deliver its mainstream services in a way that is conducive to crime prevention and safety, if the police have not developed models of effective community policing and if outreach youth work is not promoted by the youth service. The problems will be endlessly discussed and rarely resolved.**

> **Multi-agency partnerships will therefore be more effective**

> **when the preventive capacity of single agencies and departments has been developed. (Bright, 1997, p 83)**

- In *The communities we have lost and can regain*, Michael Young and Gerard Lemos (1997) point to the crucial role of social housing policy at both national and local levels. They recommend that "building communities should, along with meeting housing need be a central policy purpose of social housing" (p 105). They propose allocation systems that would recognise social as well as housing need, which would encourage families to live in proximity and the use of mutual aid compacts between social landlords and tenants.
- Charles Landry and Franco Bianchini, in *The creative city* (1995), describe new holistic approaches to city development (for an example see NEF, 1998). These involve the generation of creative responses to urban problems whether they initially present themselves in traffic management, business development, environmental/green issues, integration of excluded communities, housing regeneration or recreating city centres. This enhances working with the hard issues of physical infrastructure and space as well as the soft issues of values, aspirations, hopes and fears.

Civic entrepreneurs

Charles Leadbeater has extended his previous work on social entrepreneurs to entrepreneurial activity within the institutions themselves. His study of civic entrepreneurship, written with Sue Goss, builds on five very different exemplar case studies: West Walker, a primary school in Newcastle; the Thames Valley Police force; Kirklees Metropolitan District Council; South Somerset, a largely rural district council; and Dorset Health Authority (Leadbeater and Goss, 1998). From their case material they have drawn out a working definition,

> **Civic entrepreneurship is the renegotiation of the mandate and sense of purpose of a public organisation, which allows it to find new ways of continuing resources and people, both public and private, to deliver better social outcomes, higher social value and more social capital. (Leadbeater and Goss, 1998, pp 16-17)**

While civic entrepreneurship combines many of the elements of entrepreneurship in business and social entrepreneurship, it has to operate from within the conditions of public service institutions. They have their own particular governance structures involving accountability to politicians, rules of probity and adherence to public policy. It poses the dilemma of being innovate while staying (more or less) within the 'rules'.

The stories of two civic entrepreneurs

Box 9: Dr Angela Lennox

Ten years ago, Angela Lennox, a GP, joined a practice on one of the most deprived inner-city estates in Britain. She soon began to realise that if she was going to make an impact on the poor health of the population she would have to rethink her whole approach to being a GP, starting with her professional medical priorities.

Forty years ago the St Matthew's estate in Leicester was one of the many new estates heralded as the answer to the slum conditions and poverty of the past. Sadly, and in common with so many similar ill-fated projects, it is now more well known for its progressive social and economic decay. One survey in 1996 found it to be the second poorest estate in the UK where:

* 84% of the population of 4,000 are on housing benefit;
* the estate is held in low esteem and personal safety and theft are a continuous threat;
* 60% of children live in families headed by a lone mother;
* people leave as soon as they can resulting in 60% turnover in local schools.

In her early days she was faced with local hostility, violence to medical staff, and low turn-up to appointments; in short, a disconnection from the very patients she was supposed to help. She decided that she either had to leave for an area where patients more materially fitted perceived medical priorities, or she had to rethink her whole approach. The framework of financial and professional incentives all pointed towards a move to the more leafy suburbs. So she stayed.

The focus of the change was to start to understand the world through the eyes and experiences of local people. They saw their health needs as a result of living in stressful conditions, lack of money, fear for their own and especially their children's safety, bringing up young children alone and so on. Through this she saw that to improve health, she had to be equally interested in employment, community safety, housing, social welfare and education. "Cynics say to me that it's not my job to bring employment to the area" she explains. "And they're right – except that to improve health here I must improve employment prospects. After all, why should someone even consider the benefits of not smoking, when their needs are more basic, like security for their children?"

The transformation has been remarkable. Through a mixture of hard work, determination, vision and dogged persistence, the St Matthew's project has taken off. More than £1.7m was raised to create Prince Philip House, a multi-agency centre where a whole range of relevant services and community activity are interwoven. Primary health care operates alongside the local police office, a drug and alcohol advice centre and benefits centre, dental health, mental health, chiropody, speech and language therapy and community paediatric services. The centre has close links also to the local technical colleges, schools, housing office, residents' associations and churches.

"The key to success has been the involvement of local residents" says Angela Lennox. Also solutions to problems come from the community with professionals there to support them. A process of active learning is encouraged between residents themselves and between residents and professionals. Residents will visit other areas to learn about what they have done and how this might be applied to their situations. And of course, Angela Lennox's own 10-year journey has been one of learning and relearning every aspect of her professional role – and beyond.

Characteristically, she is also a part-time lecturer at Leicester University and places a high value on this learning experience in the training of future doctors. All Leicester University medical students spend part of their course with estate residents and support workers, developing a realistic picture of the estate's problems. (Sources: personal visit, notes and *The Guardian*)

Box 10: Norma Redfearn

In June 1986, shortly before Angela Lennox began her St Matthew's journey, Norma Redfearn became head teacher at West Walker Primary School on the outskirts of Newcastle upon Tyne. The school was facing an increasingly desperate situation. In today's terminology it was close to becoming a 'failing school'.

The school design for 250 children had a roll of around 140 – when they were there. Only six out of 18 classrooms were fully utilised. Results were poor, attendance awful.

In terms of population characteristics, West Walker bears many similarities to St Matthew's. It is an area badly hit by unemployment, poverty and dereliction, largely a result of the collapse of shipbuilding and heavy engineering. About three quarters of the pupils were on free school meals. Many of the parents were unemployed and many families headed by single mothers. As in so many similar localities, there was little social cohesion and infrastructure left; a far cry from the traditions of strong working class communities and organisations of the past. Norma Redfearn describes the situation when she started out thus: "There were no churches, no factories, no work. The school was about the only place for people to come together. If it had closed there would have been nothing".

She was determined to develop better early years educational opportunities, experiences and outcomes for her children. However, to achieve the considerable improvements she wanted, she knew that this would mean working for change both inside and outside the school.

Most parents themselves had negative experiences of education and were therefore likely to be detached from the school experience of their children. She decided that she, with her staff, had to begin to engage with the parents differently, who were frequently dispirited and lacking in self-esteem and confidence. She began talking to parents over an early morning cup of coffee. They developed a project to improve a windswept playground with the help of 'outside allies'. It succeeded and it demonstrated that parents, teachers and supporters could work together to create something better and tangible.

This led to engagement with a whole series of local agencies, housing, police, social services, adult education and so on. But like Angela Lennox, it was a mixture of the vision of better possibilities through partnership with parents and professionals and an irritating tenacity to overcome organisational and institutional blockages that brought about the longer-term change. It also involved going far beyond the traditional boundaries of 'education'.

A second early project, developed by teachers and parents working together, was to use some of the empty space in the school to create a community and adult education wing. This would have the secondary effect of limiting vandalism. For a time this was rejected by the 'wider system' because it was argued that if local people wanted adult education, they should enrol at classes in the technical college. However, a mixture of determination and the increasing support of local allies won the day. Other linked projects that have followed through parental and community involvement are:

- A cafe used by both parents and children. There is also a breakfast club sponsored and funded by Newcastle Building Society, the North Eastern Co-op, Greggs and Safeway, which provides a free breakfast and is attended by 30-40 children. She and other staff reckoned that children arriving at the school hungry were unlikely to be able to give much attention to learning.
- There is a homework club attended by about 50 children after school hours.
- The school and playground is open to children out of school hours.
- The community wing links in with a range of other local services.
- The community wing also has a library for parents, a training room and a computer room for parents and children.
- Adult education classes include keep fit, assertiveness, sewing and empathy and counselling courses particularly relating to parenting.
- Two parents, who were originally trained to provide creche facilities at the school, now run their own business employing 10 to 15 local women to provide this service across the district.
- The school has enabled parents to build lasting relationships across the community. One group of parents, who came together to improve the environment around the school, eventually went on to create a housing association which has built new housing on a derelict site.

Overall, the school has shown huge improvements in the numbers on the school roll, attendance levels and in the test results on educational attainment. (Source: Leadbeater and Goss [1998] and direct conversation)

Box 11: Summary

There are striking similarities between the paths taken by these two pioneering women working quite independently of each other and in very different professional fields. These are hopefully apparent in these two brief stories as well as in the text as a whole. But perhaps four are worthy of particular comment.

- Both worked with the big picture, realising that long-term, sustainable, significant improvements in the cases of health and education could only come about through improvements to people's self-esteem and quality of life. In turn better health and education improve quality of life. They are interdependent variables.

- Both saw real engagement and involvement of increasing numbers of community members (parents) as the essential building block. This was the key to creating linked networks of other professionals and allies working towards bringing the bigger picture into being.

- Both worked well beyond their professional remit and often found that the cultures and the reward and penalty structures of the official system worked to penalise their endeavours.

- Both stayed for the long haul having determined what kind of improvement they wanted to see. Clearly the incentive was social result rather than money. (This of course begs all sorts of questions about the likely impacts of large incentive payments such as for 'super' heads and 'super' teachers – are they simply the beneficiaries of changes in the wider system?) It also brings to mind the admonitions of Dr W. Edwards Deming, the quality guru referred to earlier. He said that Western management suffers from seven deadly diseases, one of which is job-hopping managers, another performance related pay (Deming, 1986).

Leadbeater and Goss are at pains to point out that while there are identifiable common themes in civic entrepreneurship, there are no simple blueprints. Situations are unique and each has in effect to find resolutions to the vertical/horizontal dilemma; that point where professional and managerial knowledge collides (or more normally kept apart) with both local knowledge and experience as well as the other vertically ordered knowledges of other professional systems. They write,

> **Good practice can never be bottled and applied somewhere else like an ointment. There are no one-size-fits-all, magic solutions to complex social problems. The public sector is highly heterogeneous: entrepreneurial solutions will vary for different organisations, with different histories, cultures, users and political leadership. None of the organisations profiled provide 'the right answer'. Yet each of them has achieved impressive changes and offers some important general lessons about what makes for successful civic entrepreneurship. (Leadbeater and Goss, 1998, p 18)**

They then draw out nine common themes of successful civic entrepreneurship (pp 51-60). All are important, but the first is the key to the rest.

- **Focus on outcomes not outputs:** this often means redefining narrowly-focused professional outputs. For instance, Norma Redfearn never defined her goal solely in terms of test scores and attendance. "Her school's focus is broader: to encourage entire families to become more engaged in education." By doing this, she and her colleagues achieved remarkable success in attracting pupils, and improving attendance and test results. Similarly, Angela Lennox, the Leicester GP, realised that to improve the health of her patients she had to put to one side top-down professionally-defined health goals. She needed to start with their perceptions of health need and with their involvement in meeting these. It was also apparent that poor health was inexorably woven into the fabric of high unemployment, deprivation and social breakdown. Thames Valley innovative approach to restorative justice follows a radical rethink of policing as both prevention and cure; community safety *as well as* law enforcement.

The other common themes are:

- **The quality of senior management:** they played a key role in developing the bigger picture; moving beyond departmental intent, keeping the focus outside, forging partnership working, being 'politically' adept and sticking with it. If current managers will not make the change, then ones are found who can.
- **Risk management:** doing things differently involves taking risks. Sharing risks, planning with partners – managing the risks – is an important skill. Learning from success and failure is vital.
- **Building legitimacy:** this is of particular relevance in the public services. Civic entrepreneurs have to be able to work with others to build legitimacy for their activities, otherwise their initiatives are likely to be short-lived. This will involve working with a wide variety of potential stakeholders.
- **Delivering on the ground:** entrepreneurship means moving beyond strategic thinking and partnership into tangible actions that make a social difference and can be seen to do so. Thinking and action become iterative processes of learning.
- **Working across boundaries:** this is a continuing theme so perhaps one brief example will suffice for explanation. "To create an environment in which her children could learn, Norma Redfearn needs to make sure they are properly fed and turned up on time.

The school stood a better chance of working if its physical and social environment improved. At West Walker, education is an issue which involved health, the environment, housing and social services."

- **Building capacity to create social capital:** change cannot be achieved by individual success (or charismatic leadership for that matter). Developing collaborative teamwork and close relationships with stakeholders and users creates the organisational capacity to add social value – which is social capital.
- **Seeing change as opportunity:** change is seen as a challenge. Civic entrepreneurs appear to be able to take external threats and shape them into local strategies and opportunities that address locally understood perceptions of need.
- **Embedding entrepreneurship:** as with capacity building, entrepreneurship skills need to be spread across the system. Again this calls for stickability and persistence over long periods of time. (There seems to be a corollary to this and many of the other themes. This is that job-hopping managers – to use Dr Edward Deming's description of one of Western management's deadly diseases – can never be civic entrepreneurs. The same is probably true for social entrepreneurs for similar reasons. This then raises an interesting question; how long does one have to be in a role to create civic entrepreneurship? Probably five years is a minimum, and longer, preferably.)

This section on civic entrepreneurship could equally well have been included in Chapter 4. It certainly accords well with the main themes identified there. But from our perspective it appears to link to the progression of social entrepreneurship, voluntary organisation, mutualism, care and mutual self-help, volunteerism, and capacity building that runs through this chapter so far. What is so encouraging is that the cases presented by Leadbeater and Goss represent the tip of the iceberg of this same kind of social capital building now emerging in public service institutions.

This is, of course, extremely good news, and readily observable in our own work, as well as the many examples referred to in this report so far. However, many civic entrepreneurs are having to navigate against unnecessarily strong currents of middle and senior management resistance as well as political disinterest or downright hostility. But, there are bound to be some opposing (and often valid) currents. Professionalism and appropriate specialisation bring with them many benefits. Hence reconciliation of the vertical and lateral, of professional knowledge and local knowledge, will always be required. It is not possible to have risk free entrepreneurship by rote or listed into a thousand competencies.

The unnecessary blocks to innovation/ entrepreneurship

Entrepreneurial activity is frequently downplayed or opposed. This activity takes three recognisable forms. The first of these takes the form of the many variants of 'we are already doing that' – and some genuinely think they are, when they are not. Many of the words will be in the mission and policy statements, codes of practice, protocols, service level agreements and the rest. The acid test is of course to find out from all the supposed stakeholders if there is a consistent story and what it is – especially if they can be got together to compare each other's stories.

The second form of blocking defence takes the form of "the organisation must move together as a whole, or we will encourage different service levels (and hence discrimination against some users) in different areas/institutions". This has a ring of integrity about it; it is what the public requires and is sensibly a strong public service ethic. However, given the learning and innovation that is required at all levels, change of type described here – especially reframing the professional task in terms of systemically achieved outcomes – simply cannot be achieved by the kind of top-down planning that would be required to produce even change across a system. A better way, while risking greater short-term variations in the short term (of course there will be variation already across any delivery system run by human beings) by supporting such piecemeal innovation. Facilitative leadership of the wider system/ partnership then needs to promote lateral learning from innovations, remembering that in the end everybody has to follow their own learning journeys. While there would still be variations across the system, the overall benefits for most would be considerably higher.

The third form of block is in the form of jealousy, fear, inertia or laziness, or a combination of them. This one is more difficult to get to, because the first line of defence is to use either or both of the two above as they can sound more legitimate. A further ancillary defence is "that government policy/council policy, departmental policy and so on – and information – does not allow it." (Of course it can be tricky if it really does not!) The third form of blocking can be presented in many ways; a few examples will suffice as readers will be readily able to add their own.

"It doesn't work – I once went there/know somebody there
etc."

"It's different in/at ... better staff/better users/luck with other
organisations/"

"Why are they always rocking the boat? They are just attention
seekers."

"We tried it once."

"We would, but the other departments will not entertain
cooperation. They are out to win/get our resources/offload
their problems (and sometimes they will, they are, and do!)"

The serious issue in policy terms is how can government and determined
leadership in local institutions work to create and support high levels of
civic entrepreneurship as the driving force to implementing holistic
government by creating joined-up action on the ground and the creation
of social capital? Are current ideas and proposals sufficient? Because
silo thinking is still so powerful from government departments down, it
is our belief that a fundamentally different kind of innovation is required.
This is born out of our range of previous experience, together with
work in progress on the C2M project in Bradford.

The development of the C2M project in Bradford: an outline of work in progress (Appelbee, 1998)

In 1993 the ecumenical Bradford Metropolitan Faith in the City Forum
undertook a project called 'Powerful Whispers'. This project brought
together the key decision makers within the metropolitan district and
some of the people living in four of the most disadvantaged areas of the
district.

The aim was to enable the key decision makers to hear directly from
the people living in disadvantaged communities, including local
professionals, about how life is experienced by them. The purpose was
two-fold: to demonstrate that even in hard-pressed communities there
were people with ideas who would be fitting partners for the work of
regenerating the district; and to help to widen the public debate about
the future of Bradford.

Four urban 'hearings' were held and the agenda was concerned with answering five questions:

- what was good about where people lived;
- what was not so good;
- what were local people already doing to make a difference;
- what did they see as the gaps;
- what were there hopes and fears for the future?

From the four hearings a common agenda of concerns emerged – poverty; crime; young people; race, culture and religion; consultation and decision making; and housing.

The Hearings had a profound effect on the decision makers who had sat for eight hours listening silently. One of the most powerful effects was to remind everyone concerned that they do share a common humanity and inhabit the same world. One of the 'Hearers' said: "I never realised that people want the same kinds of things as me". Another remarked that it was true that resources are scarce but he was left wondering whether the right people were being listened to when decisions were made about how those resources should be allocated.

Following the Hearings the Forum then went on to listen to the decision makers talk about how they felt about having the responsibility for trying to solve the problems. It then considered how the project might be built upon.

Out of the six common issues that emerged, the concern about the levels of consultation and decision making was the least expected. People challenged the official view that the regeneration projects which had been undertaken in the district were, bar one exception, bottom-up. They articulated clearly the damage done to the communal solidarity of the district by the competitive nature of the bidding system and criticised the decision-making process which is less than transparent. Consequently, areas of the district which are not involved in bids for SRB or European funds are left feeling even more marginalised.

On the other hand, the Powerful Whispers process also demonstrated that despite diversity there was a clear common agenda around which the increasingly separated and diverse communities of the district could be reconnected.

Through both listening exercises a picture emerged of a plethora of strategies and initiatives from the 'top', and at the 'bottom' a great deal of ad hoc activity responding directly to needs. For those at the top there was a frustration that nothing appeared to move the district forward in the way that had been hoped, and at the bottom a frustration that nobody was listening. There appeared to be a gap in the middle where the top and the bottom were failing to connect.

The report of the Bradford Commission into the Manningham riots reflected this view in a telling paragraph:

> **The critical political deficiency which we have found (in Bradford) is that there is no adequate process to link the concerns of responsible members of the public, or those working at the problems 'on the ground', with the means of participating effectively in developing local solutions. We challenge the city to produce at many levels, the leadership and the coordination which can channel the strengths of Bradford to deal with the problems we identify in this report.**

In the summer of 1997 the Faith in the City Forum moved into a new phase of work as a response to what had been heard and identified by developing a proposal for work which would attempt to meet the challenge expressed so eloquently in the Commission report. The new phase of the work is called 'The Centenary Millennium Project' (C2M) and its aim is to work in the gap between 'top-down' and 'bottom-up' – the purpose is first to bridge the gap and eventually to close it.

The central idea is to encourage as many communities in the district as possible to use the time between the City's Centenary (1997) and the other side of the Millennium (2002) to build local agendas and plans for their communities. This will take community initiatives into a further stage of development, moving from ad hoc response to need into stocktaking strengths and weaknesses of the community, prioritising need and planning responses.

In this way every community will have the opportunity to participate and create a forward momentum for themselves. Community planning will happen at an appropriate pace, not driven by funding deadlines and will put communities in a strong position to bid for funds, from all sorts of sources, in the future.

If there are a plethora of community plans, when subsequent government money does appear, then the criteria can be displayed and those with agreed plans which best fit the criteria can be put forward in a transparent manner and an open debate take place about who is chosen and why.

This work is based on a belief that every community can act, in partnership with institutions, to improve the quality of life, and that it is not dependent on ad hoc grants from government.

A concrete example of how this would work is demonstrated by an actual experience. A small local community centre in the heart of the inner city Bradford had been running very successfully for several years. The management of the centre is shared between local people, the local parish church and social services, with local people in the majority.

The management committee decided it was time to have a community survey to check out whether the services and activities currently offered were still relevant and whether new needs were emerging. A group of volunteers at the centre participated in this work. They undertook training to discover how to draw up a questionnaire, how to plan the sample, to devise the script and approach for the work. In addition, they published their findings and held an open evening for members of the community and funders so that the findings could be verbally and visually presented.

As a result of the community survey, a gap in the provision for young people was identified. With a couple of hundred pounds left from the summer trips a girls group was started which ran very successfully for several months. Supported by the community worker they put together a bid to the National Lottery Charity Board and succeeded in winning a grant of £190,000 to establish a youth project.

In order to encourage this type of bottom-up audit/planning/action work the Churches have brought together a wide-ranging partnership, backed by the major institutions within the district, to set up the project C2M. As well as inviting and resourcing communities to participate in the programme it will enable three other crucial things to happen.

The first will be to link across the district groups and communities who have common emerging agendas, plans or actions. The purpose of these links will be to share ideas and good practice. C2M has received a half million pound grant from the Millennium Commission to make such grants to individuals, or two or three people working together on the C2M programme. These grants will carry a requirement to participate in small action learning groups with other recipients. In this way people from very different communities will become connected through common concerns and actions and from this it is anticipated that people across Bradford District will experience first hand that within diversity they share a common humanity.

It is almost impossible in Bradford to celebrate the wonderful diversity which exists within the district and wider society. Perhaps it is because diversity, detached from any understanding that people share common values and concerns, is frightening because it highlights difference, allowing people to view each other only as aliens. When people are confident that some key values and concerns are held in common, then they can believe that diversity is something to safely celebrate and enjoy.

The second task for C2M is working with institutions to increase their capacity to partner more effectively with communities. For the last 40 years local government was confident in its role as the key provider of services for local communities. While the last 10 years has seen an erosion of this role it has only led to an increase in a 'quango' culture and the consolidation of a 'those at the top know best' mentality, despite the occasional rhetoric of community partnership. Expertise has been seen as resting with the professionals.

There is a need for a shift in this culture and this is recognised by the institutions within Bradford and is reflected in the manner in which the institutions have approached the C2M project. Initially, and understandably cautious, there is now very good support which has been demonstrated both in terms of 'cash and kind' donations but more importantly, in the amount of time which various officers have been allowed to contribute to the development of the project. C2M does not seek to blame local institutions for the challenges which Bradford faces, but rather to acknowledge that everyone is having to invent new responses to a rapidly changing economic and social scene and to seek to facilitate the new relationships needed to address that changing reality.

A great deal of time within the two-year development stage of the project has been spent in building relationships with key officers and politicians within the institutions. This has been critical for the successful roll out of the project, and not least for the first part of C2M's planned work with those institutions.

This first major piece of work will be a two-day Whole System's event in February 1999 and will involve the key agencies involved in the Health Action Zone, the Crime and Disorder Partnership and 'regeneration' work within the district. The aim of the event is to enable a cross-section of workers from the agencies – from front-line staff to executive directors – to explore together their current experiences of partnership working, both with each other and with the community, the obstacles and problems and to develop an agenda for action and change.

It had been intended originally that the event would focus exclusively on partnerships between institutions and communities. However, the volume of initiatives flowing from central government has put huge pressures on even the most robust of partnerships and so the quality of partnering between institutions and agencies in the new climate has had to be included.

The proposal by C2M that such an event be held was met with enthusiastic approval by the institutions concerned and indeed coincided with their own plans and thinking, particularly with that of the HAZ partnership. This has meant that instead of C2M laying on an event to which the others come, there is now a genuine sense of joint ownership. This feels particularly right in terms of the role C2M believes it right to play ie that of facilitator.

The third task is to enable the information and good practice being generated at the grass roots to be gathered and passed on to those who have responsibility for thinking strategically about services and plans for the district.

From the very outset of the development of C2M it was recognised that the project had to be clearly independent, while having a membership which included individuals, community groups, voluntary sector and institutions and the backing of the major institutions of the district. Three advantages have accrued from this independence.

Firstly, C2M is winning the support and participation of communities. From discussions which took place through Powerful Whispers and beyond, it was obvious that the formal institutions such as 'the council' would not easily be able to initiate such a project because they are viewed as having agendas which do not always coincide with that of local people, a case of 'us' and 'them'.

Secondly, C2M is able to act as a risk bearer thereby making possible the participation of institutions who would not otherwise attempt such work. The agenda undertaken by C2M constitutes a risky venture. It is hugely ambitious, wide-ranging and capable of falling flat on its face – this was especially true in its early stages of development. Even to those committed and involved it seemed a highly crazy project. Risk taking is antithetical to institutions, indeed their function is to embody all that makes for stability. C2M enables both institutions and communities to participate in necessary risk taking without having to bear the consequences. C2M does this on their behalf.

Thirdly, it provides an external pressure to both institutions and communities to take action which otherwise might be avoided, delayed or sidelined. An example of this is the planned two day Whole Systems event with the institutions. Individual officers within the institution had identified, up to two years ago, that there was a need for such work to be undertaken using the same methodology, but somehow it never seemed possible to move the idea forward. Eventually it probably would have happened especially as it had finally been included in a corporate action plan. However, C2M as an independent group, has been able to help move this process forward by making a concrete proposal, inviting the institutions to act with us to make it happen now.

Through this project it is hoped to enhance the ability of the citizens of Bradford District and its institutions to dismantle the current barriers of race, class and culture to learn from each other as together they take hold of the future. In effect, to create a learning district. In this way community life can be reconstructed and strengthened, widening the opportunities for participation.

Notes

[1] Watford Council are pioneering a 'Better government for older people' pilot which recognises older people as an untapped resource. The project embraces the Time Dollars Institute's methodology of using Time as Currency as a way of encouraging co-production and reciprocity.

[2] See Mulgan and Landry, 1995.

[3] Knight and Stokes, 1996. Civil society is defined by Cohen and Arato, 1992, as "a sphere of social interaction between economy and the state, above all of the intimate sphere (especially the family), the sphere of associations (especially voluntary associations), social movements and forms of public communications". A deficit in civil society implies the lack of this social interaction.

[4] Skinner, 1997. In the introduction Steve Skinner defines capacity building as "Development work that strengthens the ability of community organisations and groups to build their structures, systems, people and skills so that they are better able to define and achieve their objectives and engage in consultation and planning, manage community projects and take part in partnerships and community enterprises. It includes aspects of training, organisational and personal development and resource building, organised in a planned and self-conscious manner, reflecting the principles of empowerment and equality."

SEVEN

Improving sustainable quality of life: the benchmark for Best Value

While the ravages of the 1950s and 1960s have fortunately abated, there is still not sufficient understanding of how a sense of place can be created, maintained or recreated. The debate about urban sustainability highlights the links between the natural, physical, social, cultural, political and economic environments and is thus encouraging holistic thinking. Yet our institutions for decision-making about cities are still largely based on rigid functional specialisations, without sufficient sharing and co-operation between different departments, disciplines and sectors. (Landry and Bianchini, 1995, pp 15–16)

Government consultation has been taking place on radical plans to strengthen local democracy and community leadership through stronger community involvement in community planning. This has resulted in the publication of the White Paper *Modern local government: In touch with the people* (DETR, 1998). This will result in new duties being placed on local authorities to promote the economic, social and environmental well-being of their areas. Clearly this could be consistent with the discussion in Chapters 4 and 5 about change that works. However, it would need to take seriously the requirement for locally-led capacity building and very different sets of relationships that currently exist between many providers and service beneficiaries. We develop a series of proposals in Chapter 9 that are designed to develop both community and institutional capacities as the basis for changing the relationship between citizens, communities and institutions. This chapter now looks at a series of linked issues that are inextricably linked with people's quality of life in communities.

The previous three chapters – 4, 5 and 6 – focused on social and, to a limited extent, economic well-being. This chapter will look more closely at environmental well-being and its links to the social and economic. The uniting theme is 'quality of life' and the means of obtaining this should then become the benchmark of Best Value, the obligation being placed on lateral authorities, and potentially on other public bodies, to improve the quality, efficiency and effectiveness of service delivery for the public.

Local Agenda 21: the path of long-term economic well-being

Sustainability: the vision[1]

Following the Brundtland Report (1987), talk of sustainable development began in earnest even though the term had already been in use for about a decade. The widespread use of the term marked an important step forward for its history, because it meant that the debate moved away from the narrower agendas of conservation, poverty, human rights, economic growth or GDP and started to focus on the *inter-relation* between environmental, social and economic agendas.

In talking about definitions of sustainable development, it is useful to distinguish between *sustainability*, which is a goal or vision, and *sustainable development*, which is the means or process for achieving the vision. This is useful in part because the goal of sustainability is easier to define than the process for getting there.

Agenda 21 gives one useful definition:

> **The goal of national sustainable development strategies should be to ensure socially responsible economic development while protecting the resource base and the environment for the benefit of future generations. (UNCED, 1992)**

The Brundtland Report introduces the important, integrating notion of 'quality of life'.

> **Sustainable Development is development that enhances the quality of life for all, without compromising the ability of future generations to meet their own needs. (World Commission on Environment and Development, 1987)**

Jonathon Porritt offers one of the simplest definitions:

> **Sustainability is the capacity for continuance.**

But perhaps it is expressed most simply and elegantly by the permaculture movement:

Earth care, people care, fair shares. (Mollison, 1990)

For some, the notion of sustainable development has become debased through overuse (at our last count, in February 1996, there were over 280 definitions in circulation). Others have suggested that the term 'sustainable development', in which sustainable is a mere adjective to a denominating noun, be replaced by 'developing sustainability', in which sustainabililty becomes the noun and so takes on the appropriate focus as a new institutional structure to be created through economic (and other) processes (McGonigle, 1989).

The government response

The government has launched central and local government guidance on LA21 (DETR, 1998b). Speaking at the launch, John Prescott, the Deputy Prime Minister said,

> **We aren't just concerned with cleaning up litter and dog dirt, recycling waste and cutting air pollution. We are in the business of making lasting improvements in the quality of life of local people and their children – working to meet environmental *and* economic and social goals. (John Prescott, Deputy Prime Minister, DETR Press Release, 14 January 1998)**

Writing to all leaders and chief executives of local authorities in England, Sir Jeremy Beecham, Chairman of the Local Government Association (LGA), in support of the new guidance, defines sustainable development as "ensuring a better quality of life for everyone, now and for generations to come. It encompasses environmental, social and economic goals" (LGA, letter from Sir Jeremy Beecham to all leaders and chief executives of local authorities in England, 14 January 1998). Local authorities are required to review their existing strategies, or if they do not already have one, develop one by December 2000.

In his letter, Sir Jeremy makes three further statements of particular relevance:

Local Agenda 21 is the process of agreeing and implementing

local sustainable development action plans for the 21st Century in partnership with the local community. It should not be a separate 'project', but rather be *built into everything the local authority does*, like financial probity and value for money. It must become a mainstream activity. The main challenge of the next few years will be to place Local Agenda 21 at the centre of the initiative to promote good local governance.

Producing a Local Agenda 21 strategy encourages councils to listen to local views and allows them to translate sustainable development goals into local action. Local authorities are best placed to identify local priorities and galvanise local participation so as to make the best use of the resources and enthusiasm available in their area.

I believe that the process of working towards sustainable development and thereby setting a corporate direction and identifying priorities in close participation with the local community, will also bring direct benefits to councils by helping deliver a number of important policies. The new frameworks and processes that will flow from the *joint central and local government agenda to revitalise local government – for example on Best Value, local community leadership, and democratic renewal* – will in turn provide opportunities to support and deliver the objectives of Local Agenda 21.

[Emphasis reproduced from actual letter.]

On the face of it, this is heartening. The strategic connections are made and there is encouragement to work towards the development of action plans in partnership with the community, of identifying priorities in close participation with the local community, of listening to local views. But what will this mean in practice? How will action be integrated at local level, across internal authority departments, let alone with the myriad other agencies? Will partnership with community be of the type being advocated here, the outcome of community capacity building? Or will it be a series of individual silo-based consultations when priorities and plans remain the possession of the professionals? Is the message one of enlightened managerial consumerism or is it driven from the requirement to relate services to the renewal of community?

Again, on the positive side, it links the definition of sustainability to the continuance of the quality of life, close to the Brundtland definition. It ties in with the purpose of this report in seeing regeneration, local community renewal and environmental sustainability as a single, multi-faceted entity. Further, it links LA21 to the revitalisation of local government, and in turn to Best Value, local community leadership, and democratic renewal.

What will be critical in practice will be how and who defines the meaning and nature of local community leadership and democratic renewal and how these in turn 'frame' Best Value, or whether Best Value 'frames' them. If the lessons of research on regeneration are to be incorporated, as indeed they should, then local community leadership must be the outcome of capacity and given recognition in new frameworks of local governance. This will not be a route that will readily appeal to all local politicians or professionals because it will severely upset many conventional understandings of power and status. It will mean using power very differently but we argue, far more productively. This potential conflict follows directly from the issues discussed previously, particularly in Chapter 2.

In essence, local authorities and their other (particularly) public sector partners may either:

- Open up and address these challenges to the conventional (control and command) uses of power and authority. Legitimised authority (political) through democratic mandate and executive authority over resources are increasingly used to widen the circles of inclusivity. Institutions and communities become interactive.
- Or do what many have always done; adopt the new rhetoric of change while conducting business largely as usual. Detecting this by external audit still remains surprisingly difficult. This is largely because of the lack of awareness of the interconnectedness of the issues and therefore indicators of holistic outcomes.

Most encouraging of all, the LGA has launched its pathfinders project under the heading of the New Commitment to Regeneration (1998). This requests authorities to bid for pathfinder status through developing effective processes for regeneration partnerships in ways which could support the key ideas being developed in this report.

The horizontal and vertical integration of planning systems[2]

Great stress has been placed on communities being increasingly involved in the auditing, planning and taking action around their own perceptions of need. This capacity building towards widening social networks of engagement is the basis for rebuilding social capital and for participating in wider locality planning with institutions and agencies. It is also clear that this needs to embrace LA21; it is part and parcel of the same whole.

But this raises a series of wider issues and questions:

- How will these local neighbourhood-driven planning processes link to associated issues of land-use, transport, environment, waste management, health and housing planning for example? – the horizontal links.
- And how will these local neighbourhood planning activities that increasingly involve communities and front-line service providers and other local stakeholders working together, connect with the district-wide plans of local authorities and the emerging Regional Development Agencies (RDAs)? – the vertical links.

The basis of the current planning system originates from the great 1947 postwar Town and Country Planning Act. It has been the principle means of guiding public and private investment and arbitrating between seemingly irreconcilable interests and priorities. In many respects these existing planning processes lie at the heart of democratic values and the operation of local governance. "In every planning decision, someone benefits, someone loses, and someone pays" (Gavron, 1998a).

But the Act seemed to limit planning systems to a narrow focus on land-use, and this in turn has led to an inevitable lowering of planners' horizons. Landry and Bianchini put it thus,

> **One symptom of the narrowness of planners' horizons is the fact that they find it very hard to focus on desires rather than needs. According to our definition, a need is an objectifiable entity: 'I need a lamp post outside my front door'; 'I need a more frequent bus service'; 'I need more policeman on the beat in the town centre'. A desire, by contrast, involves your subconscious, a personal engagement, dreams and feelings, and the atmosphere and feeling of a place. (Landry and Bianchini, 1995, p 16)**

The impact of this has been to make planning processes remote, 'official' and top-down. They frequently get a bad press associated with the application of bureaucratic professional views that may seem antithetical to local wishes and 'common sense'. The process seems designed to foster either apathy or anger. In part this is a consequence of attempting to reconcile the unreconcilable. But it is also because it has become detached from the people's (and local communities') wishes and desires as well as from many other planning concerns. The avoidance of emotion, particularly of feelings of frustration and anger, will inevitably lead to cathartic discharge at some time in the future.

The disconnection of land-use planning from other forms of planning causes further difficulties. Nicky Gavron writes,

> *... the planning system did not include economic planning, housing, transport, financial planning or newer concerns about the environment.* **Of course, it dealt with the land-use side of the economy, housing and transport, but it** *did not co-ordinate them into a single process.* **Nor did it tie policy, strategy and mechanisms together into a comprehensive package.**
>
> *It created a quasi-judicial process seen as separate and discrete from areas of policy and action with which it is intrinsically linked.* **This ... is a fatal flaw and the cause of wasted energy and inefficiencies which dog local government. (Gavron, 1998b, p 24)**

[Emphasis reproduced from the original text.]

It is axiomatic following the arguments in this report that the basic building block of 'planning' (as in people coming together to build common pictures of the future, rather than just the plans themselves) must be at the neighbourhood level. It has to be participative in ways that are quite different from the normal professionally-led adversarial enquiries and local 'consultations'. The core of neighbourhood plans will need to be land-use and transport based. But this should also clearly link into the very specific concerns, needs and aspirations of local people and their reconnections with mainstream service and other stakeholders around the agendas that emerge from these. It is via these processes of engagement that localities can re-engage with *both* town and country planning processes as well as with the wider worlds of local governance and civic society. Building on the work of Robert Putnam (see Chapter 3, p 53), we suggest that the institutions could start to work differently based on the proposals and recommendations we make, and that these differences would have a significant impact on localities and their long-term quality of life and well-being. But, in the long run, the quality of our institutions, democracy and governance is dependent upon the rebuilding of our civic society. The key to this is going local. Local must come home. This needs to be the rationale for improving both the competence and legitimacy of local services and their governance. It could form the basis for a new decentralising settlement between central and local government (Mulgan and 6, 1996).

Benchmarking Best Value

In its operation, Best Value (together with the political fixation on hospital waiting lists) will make or break the conditions for joined-up action on the ground and therefore any moves towards holistic government. Simply defined, Best Value is an obligation on a local authority to continually search to improve the quality, efficiency and effectiveness of all its activities and service delivery for the public. Currently two police forces along with 37 local authorities have been selected to pilot Best Value. As such, they are exempt from current CCT legislation. Best Value is now set to replace CCT in future years. It is a concept that could be applied to all public bodies.

In the initial phase the government has been very successful in attracting authorities to bid for pilot status – a far cry from the resistance to previous governments' CCT legislation. Some were clearly drawn as a way of 'avoiding' CCT obligations. But it is clear that Best Value could be more rigorous and demanding than CCT in the long run. There is little doubt that the government sets great store by it. It is widely suggested that this could be local government's last chance following the Conservatives' private discussions about whether to abolish the current arrangements around the time of the 1992 elections. Hilary Armstrong, the local government minister, "has warned councils that the very legitimacy of local government rests on the success of Best Value" (*Local Government Chronicle*, 12 December 1997). And no doubt this will equally apply to subsequent national initiatives for the renewal of local governance. Thus the pressure on local authorities to perform has never been higher, while at the same time there are clearly doubts at the highest levels of its capability to do so. It therefore seems inevitable that the government will retain central powers to intervene and temporarily take over 'failing authorities'.

Whose Best Value is it anyway?

At its simplest, the value placed on a product or service is very much a subjective judgement placed upon it by an individual user or customer. For the private sector this is a relatively simple matter, once the initial concept has been understood. However, this becomes more complex where a number of services, typically across agencies, impact upon individuals, groups from across the community (children, elderly people, for example) or whole communities themselves. From any of these perspectives, the collective impact of services may vary considerably from highly effective to negligible. Much will depend upon whether individual services are judged to meet need – personal and/or collective – and whether they act in tandem to meet this need. In these contexts the pursuit of Best Value within each local authority department is unlikely, of itself, to address these more complex situations. Sustaining the development of quality of life will require that the outcomes used to identify Best Value are holistic and community-based. How the initial concept of Best Value is framed is of key importance in tackling the wicked issues, renewing local governance, rebuilding community and social cohesion and achieving sustainability. The varying possibilities of framing Best Value will need to be embraced within the methodologies employed in the evaluation studies of Best Value pilots and longer term, through the audit regimes that will be set up to monitor progress.

Given that in conceptual terms at least, Best Value could be applied across all services commissioned across the public sector, then these issues about measuring value for money can be applied across all services and not just those of local government. In any case, many services outside local government contribute to the package of services received and experienced at the level of both individual and neighbourhood.

The matrix in Table 2 presents a way of differentiating between many ways of determining value. Some are similar and will overlap in practice. Each is equally valid given it is used in its appropriate context.

Table 2: Best Value benchmarking matrix

	Individual user	Individual citizens	User/target group focus Communities of interest/concern	Neighbourhood/ local community focus
Consultation				
Participation				

Consultation and participation (how are people involved?)

These words are frequently used as though they are interchangeable. For the purpose of argument here, there is a need to make a clear distinction between them, although at the boundaries they frequently overlap.

Consultation processes are designed to elicit views and feelings about services, needs, proposals and so on from a sample of those affected. The information gained is then used to make decisions and/or judgements about those services, needs, and proposals in the formal professional and political systems of the delivery organisation(s) concerned. This 'local knowledge', gained from direct experience in a specific context, inevitably loses the richness of meaning it had for those to whom it belonged.

> As electricity is hard to store and best used as it is generated, so any knowledge, extracted from the context in which it is created, quickly loses power and meaning. Stored and transported necessarily in a few words, which function mainly as an index, the indescribable mass of data essential to making sense of the situation is not recorded and is quickly lost. The problem of professional knowledge ('P' or 'programmed knowledge' in action learning terminology) is that it is a generalised storehouse based on the resolution of past problems and lacking sensitivity to difference. (Pedler, forthcoming, p 17)

However, the accumulation of such data and its assimilation into professional knowledge can be extremely valuable for both benchmarking and improving many services. But those providing the information remain detached and distanced for decision-making processes that determine future service allocation, quantity and standards. Nor will they know how their views have been used, if at all. For the consumers of many services, this will be a matter of little consequence. Very few users of a leisure centre would want to be involved with its management.

Participation processes, on the other hand, draw views and feelings into, or very much closer to, the decision-making processes. Whether at the level of individual, user group or community group, there is likely to be much more dialogue between professionals and users and in some cases participation in the decision-making processes. New meanings and understandings are being made together, often 'in the same room'. This is what increasingly takes place in the successful regeneration processes described in Chapter 4.

On the boundaries, consultative and participative processes overlap. Because there can ultimately be no hard and fast dividing line between the two, this inevitable overlap does provide the means for dressing up what are in fact consultation processes, as empowerment. For instance, the fact that one or two residents attend a SRB board meeting held in the town hall, or elected members and officers address and respond to questions from citizens in community meetings, does not mean that this can be described as empowerment. One would need to know a great deal more about the wider context of interaction between professional and local. Far too often in such gatherings the politicians and officers dominate the proceedings in terms of agenda and contribution. The ethos is telling and selling rather than of joint enquiry. The culture and style of the town hall is taken to the community, rather than the reverse. It is programmatic rather than organic. It is the way of keeping control; of appearing to change but hanging on to the culture of the status quo.

Individuals and communities (who is involved?)

This provides the other axis for the matrix and can be divided into four positions.

1. *Individual users* can be canvassed for their views by a whole series of mechanisms – surveys, focus groups, questionnaires, suggestion schemes, complaint procedures and so on. They may also be directly involved in decisions that affect them; participation in case conferences being a good example.

2. *Individual citizens* similarly may be canvassed for their views. The difference here is that they are likely to be asked about a range of issues and services that impact upon them. This may start to provide a different picture covering shortfalls and overlaps that individual service surveys cannot elicit. Depending on the method, range and scope of the survey method used, much data may also be revealed about 'community conditions' and the impact of services and environmental issues far wider than the service coverage of the local authority or any other agency. This will inevitably start to raise wider holistic issues of value.

   Citizens' juries and panels may be used in either of the above categories despite the use of the word citizen – beware the snake oil! This will depend upon the context and focus of the issue or topic chosen. Does this lie firmly within the remit of an individual service or does it span a much wider range? But because these mechanisms involve very limited numbers of individuals they remain very much in the individualistic (rather than community) frame of reference. However, they do move from consultation to participation. Individuals are drawn into the system to throw new light on the professional task. The danger is that they end up being captured by the professional agenda.

   There is a very real danger that one or two techniques – 'Planning for Real' and say, citizens' juries – become *the solution* (answering the search of a new 'one best way') for modernising local government. Undoubtedly they can be a very useful means of addressing some difficult and contentious issues, but from the perspective of this report, they do not take us very far along the capacity building and developing sustainable quality of life agendas. In disturbing times there is usually a rush to find the new wonder pill to ease the painful symptoms of distress. Citizens' juries may be destined for this role and end as little more than useful bolt-ons to the status quo. (And rather expensive too.)

3. *User/target groups and communities of interest/concern* are increasingly being used to inform groups about services, provide support and ascertain needs. A good example of this is the increasing use of forums bringing together professionals across agencies with members of specific client groups and/or carers – elderly people, disabled people, particular forms of illness and so on. Given continuity of the process and an opening up of dialogue, consultation is then likely to move towards involvement with holistic implications for all the

agencies concerned. Taking the example of carers, the boundaries between the organisation and both clients and carers becomes more open. Carers may attend training programmes provided by the agencies in aspects of care as well as lifting and handling and back care.

4. *Neighbourhood/local community focus* is being increasingly advocated by the funders of regeneration. But, as has been stressed throughout this report, rhetoric often runs a long way in front of practice. There is, however, a mass of good practice and experimentation on the ground but little understood in the higher echelons of the managerial and political cadres of the delivery agencies and partnership bodies. Crucially this success is dependent upon moving from consultation to fuller participation. In more deprived neighbourhoods, at least, this is the essential foundation to curative and sustainable local governance and improvement to the quality of life. This is where the real challenge lies, for local government in particular.

Preventative government: the third dimension?

It could be argued that prevention should be added as a third dimension. To resonate with the goals of holistic government, prevention and sustainability will need to be key benchmarks for Best Value. The two-dimensional model above assumes these, especially around the convergence of user groups/neighbourhood focus and genuine participation. It also provides for a simpler model. But the addition of a third dimension would make prevention and sustainability more explicit.

Positioning on the matrix

There are still many organisations who do the minimum necessary consultation and participation. As this is usually to meet the requirements of external bodies – or this is how it is perceived – little thought has been given to how such data could be incorporated into internal standards of benchmarking. Further, because the development of performance indicators has been largely set externally by the Audit Commission and other regulatory bodies, local government has less experience of developing its own benchmarking standards, especially those that embrace measures of holistic effectiveness. In terms of the internal development of benchmarking Best Value standards, most local authorities are barely off the ground – or on the matrix. This will be the key challenge of moving from the CCT regime, if Best Value is to be the vehicle through which significant parts of the government's agenda are to be implemented.

The Best Value benchmarking matrix is designed to open up and begin the process of clarifying the significant parameters involved. No one position on the matrix is inherently superior to any other. It depends upon overall decisions about purposes, priorities and practical decisions based upon evidence of what will work at the level of concrete implementation.

In some localities there may be (apparently) little need for, or interest in, a community focus. Most people may be perfectly happy with the current level of social cohesion and community activity, being already involved within a number of social networks extending into wider communities of interest. Their requirements for reliable, efficient local services can be met – and measured – through occasional individual user consultation. Some may want a little higher level involvement with the local primary school for example, but each service can be seen as being engaged independently. Even so, environmental concerns, fear of crime, and an ageing population are increasingly likely to raise more locality and user group concerns and issues across a range of communities.

The basic hypothesis put forward here is that to address realistically the vital issues of developing and improving sustainable quality of life – the agenda for curative local governance – then most local authorities and their partner agencies will have to move the balance of their focus downwards and to the right. This has significant consequences for the whole ethos, style, culture, direction and leadership for all the organisations concerned, but especially local government.

The management of change agenda

The management of change matrix in Table 3 (pp 135-6) illustrates some significant features of the potential change agendas according to the positioning on the Best Value matrix. It distinguishes two broad positions taken from the Best Value matrix; firstly, one towards the top left, of consultation with individual users and secondly, one towards the bottom right of participation with user groups and communities of interest/concern/neighbourhood. It then looks at the different organisational change implications along a number of dimensions depending on the organisation's positioning against these two 'broad' orientations. It illustrates what will be paradigmatic shift for much of current public management, especially local government, if it is to take the necessary lead.

The implementation of holistic government and improving the quality of life will require institutions to work with holistic and systemic principles of change and embrace working with communities. Best Value can clearly be a significant driver of this. But if it remains silo driven, then in the search for efficiency and effectiveness it may be more likely to impede the many other efforts aiming for such improvement and change. It is a delightfully clear and elegant concept, but its value in implementing holistic government is entirely dependent on the policy and organisational choices made about how it is to be used.

'Better by far' – but better for whom?

The Audit Commission's Best Value management paper, *Better by far – Preparing for Best Value* (Audit Commission, 1998), does not make particularly encouraging reading from the perspectives emerging in this report.

On the plus side, it does make passing reference to the 'wicked issues' and the need for authorities' plans to link in with those of other public services, like the NHS and with partnership initiatives tackling specific local problems such as 'youth offending teams' (Audit Commission, 1998, p 23). It also talks of the need for similar coordination and partnership within authorities. Local Performance Plans (LPPs) will be the recommended vehicle for putting together the "variety of statutory and non-statutory plans which the authority prepares" (p 23). LPPs will in turn reflect community planning processes expressed through Community Plans.

However, the sole mode of public engagement advocated is consultation and the predominant ethos is consumerist. The paper talks of 'topics' on which councils might seek to engage with local people (p 40). Both the purposes of consultation and the uses to which the data is put remain firmly within institutional control. There is discussion of the advantages and disadvantages of four different approaches to service selection: service-based, area-based, customer-focused, and cross-cutting issues (potentially a 'wicked issues' approach) (pp 45-7).

Given the overall style and tenor of the document, it is difficult to see much enthusiasm or encouragement being extended beyond service-based and consumer-focused approaches. That is, other than perhaps to the necessary gestures in the direction of more problematic issues, and the government's public policy declaration for integrated approaches to social problems. There is no reference to, or discussion of, the fundamental issues of social exclusion, building social cohesion and capacity, and the need to radically readdress mainstream service provision and delivery as central to social and economic regeneration.

From the bigger picture perspectives taken in this report, it is difficult to avoid the conclusion that the Audit Commission is currently operating on a slightly modified, but extended, version of its more traditional approaches to CCT. And in the end it will be its regulatory approach, together with the ever growing and strengthening silo-based inspectorates, which will set the conditions within which local joined-up action will either flourish, or, as first indicators appear to suggest, continue to struggle against the dominant tide. Unless the Social Exclusion Unit (and government cross-departmental committees) addresses the issues of audit and regulation, it will rapidly lead towards its own institutional social exclusion. Is the history of JASP about to be repeated? (See Chapter 2, Box 2.)

Two quotes from the Audit Commission's report perhaps best illustrate its institutional producer orientation – despite its protestations to be user/customer driven. In talking briefly about the advantages and disadvantages of a 'wicked issues' approach it says,

> **Typically, what the public says it wants from its local council is action against 'crime and disorder' rather than improvements to named services... The disadvantage of a 'wicked issues' approach again concern performance monitoring, together with the added concern that a local council may only have limited ability to act directly on the issue in question. It may fall more readily within the remit of another agency, or even require regional – or national – level intiatives. (Audit Commission, 1998, p 45)**

Precisely. Surely this is a statement of the institutional problem to be solved, rather than a disadvantage – unless the issue is seen from within the dominant institutional perspective.

Notes

[1] We are grateful to our colleague John Colvin for contributing this section. [John Colvin, Sustainable Futures, Gigg Mill, Old Bristol Road, Nailsworth, Gloucestershire GL6 OJP.]

[2] We are greatly indebted to the ideas of Councillor Nicky Gavron for the analysis in this section. Nicky Gavron is Chair of the LGA Planning Committee. [Nicky Gavron, 17 Broadlands Road, London N6 4AE.]

Table 3: Whole System Best Value management of change matrix

	From individual user consultation	Towards user group/ neighbourhood participation
Engagement with the public	Largely consultative and departmental/silo-based. Strong boundaries maintained between departments and service users. 'Local knowledge' appropriated into the professional/political arena.	More participative and involving and increasingly group focused. Flexible according to context. A weakening of the boundaries between the parts of the organisation and between the organisation and the wider populations.
Benchmarking and types of measures used	Necessary to conform to the Best Value regime. Economy. Efficiency. Output-based. Outcome measures developed at the level of individual service users. The drive to develop Best Value benchmarks driven by external requirement.	Similar, but growing requirement for effective measures that link to: • holistic outcomes • community agendas • sustainability (soft as well as hard). The drive to develop Best Value benchmarks internally driven because of increasing clarity of purpose.
'Tackling the 'wicked issues'	"What are those?" "It's largely down to the police" (or the health authority or education or 'regeneration'). The issues are seen as 'out there'.	Linked to the clarity of purpose above. Issues are 'in here' and are linked to decisions about local delivery of mainstream services, strategic and local partnership etc.
Capacity building and sustainability	Things to do with regeneration, European funding and LA21. Important, but localised in impact and largely outside mainstream funding. Make up for cuts. "I have been to seminars/conferences about them."	Again, seen as essential to implementing the new agenda. An important means, integral to the above in achieving success.
Perception of power and dependency	Power as a zero-sum phenomena. Empowerment means giving up power. Managerialist/consumerist approach to Best Value. Incremental adjustments to the status quo. If dependency is an issue, it relates largely to welfare benefits.	Power viewed as the capacity for people to exercise productive influence both inside and beyond the organisation's formal boundaries. Thus the amount of power across the whole system can be increased and potential released for sustaining improvement collaboratively. Altering the dependency relationship seen as crucial in developing neighbourhood-based partnerships.
Role of elected members	Manage, oversee and often control the system. Democratic mandate gives right to speak on behalf of citizens and communities, but increasing acceptance of need for customer satisfaction data and some consultation.	Strategise and taking the broad political overview of the district's needs. Increasingly see democratic mandate as the focus for acting inclusively; being a channel for identifying wider community views.

Table 3: ...contd

	From individual user consultation	Towards user group/ neighbourhood participation
Role of regeneration projects	Bringing in much needed extra resources, especially in deprived areas. Focus on efficient management and monitoring of the resources involved.	Bringing in extra resources to act as a catalyst for local capacity building and effective neighbourhood partnerships linking mainstream delivery to local agendas and participation.
Inter-agency partnership	Necessary to conform to new government requirements. Useful for keeping in touch with the district overview. Necessary for gaining external funding and delivery of important service programmes like community care. The important work is done in supporting – in being seen to support – bids for funding etc. Work is largely done when the application is successful.	Partnership seen as essential to maintaining the social, economic and environmental overview. Creating the conditions across the agencies for effective local partnership working. The work begins when 'the bid' is successful. Maintaining *strategic* direction of the whole.
Management ethos	Efficiency, economy, control. Managing each initiative as a discrete element and breaking each down into ordered and clearly defined parts. The organisation as machine as the guiding metaphor. Dominance of professional, managerial and traditional political values and perspectives.	Effectiveness, seeing the bigger picture. Developing inclusive social strategies so many can see the whole. The organisation as learning system as the guiding metaphor. Professional, managerial and political perspectives both modified and developed through dialogue with each other in openly addressing community agendas.
Managing change	Planned top-down by appropriate staff experts. Implemented through programmatic procedures. • restructuring • briefing • incentives and targets • top-down initiatives • training. While there is often much talk of changing the culture, the means chosen to conduct the change are largely similar to those used in the past.	Top-down strategic direction and inclusive vision building. External change agenda used as a stimulus to address key local and district issues. Use of organic and holistic change methodologies where 'structure' follows 'process'. Widespread use of • cross-functional, task-aligned teams drawing in all the stakeholders/working with diversity • Organisation Development (OD) • whole systems approaches to change • action learning • large-scale intervention methods • enquiry groups • continuing reflective learning.

EIGHT

Joined-up action on the ground: six key issues that have to be addressed

"The people who are in power have just sat back and watched it get like it; the people who live there have sat back expecting the people who run the borough to do something about it." (Walsall resident quoted in Neighbourhood Governance in the Borough of Walsall)

"I fear the professional cultures of people working in housing and social services will militate against the government's proposals. Working as a housing officer in a deprived area, I witness every day the appalling 'top-down' managerial approach. Any money that comes our way has been 'spent', regardless of local opinion. This is coupled with backbiting between different departments. Mr Blair needs to change the cultures of those who work in the target estates, not just those who live in them." (Name and address supplied, letter to *The Guardian* on 18 September 1998 in response to the Prime Minister's launch of the Social Exclusion Unit's report, *Bringing Britain together*)

The unfolding public service agenda provides superb opportunities for creating purposeful change that can substantially improve the quality of life for many – especially for those in more disadvantaged communities. In addition, many in the public services are beginning to recognise these exciting new possibilities. We are clearly on the threshold of developing for the future radically new approaches of dealing with the key public service outcomes that concern the population.

However, the historical legacy must also be recognised and dealt with, if this promise is to materialise. There are six key issues that have to be addressed if the goal of joined-up action is not to be subverted into so much joined-up rhetoric. These are of equal significance to both policy formulation, and to implementors and practitioners. They are drawn from the preceding chapters and highlighted because of their potential significance (because they draw upon this material, this chapter has not been referenced).

Developing evidence-based approaches to change: using the research

Perhaps the saddest and most frustrating aspect of so much change effort is the widespread ignorance of what works – this is all the more poignant where social and economic regeneration initiatives are concerned. In part, this may be because much of the evidence, not surprisingly, points to multi-pronged, multi-agency interventions into complex systems of causation. Therefore, it can be easily read – if read at all – as falling into other people's domains. Much of it can be seen as 'something to do with community development' and therefore separate from the components of service delivery. It will be difficult to move forward until a critical mass of service deliverers recognise the impact of their services, both historically and currently, on communities.

Further specific areas of professional knowledge are built upon the accumulation of past theory and practice. For many tasks, professional skills and specialisations are both valuable and essential. But there are also in-built dangers of working cultures that become inner-focused leading to 'the not-invented-here syndrome'. This is all the more so when linked into predominating Fordist and Taylorist managerial and political systems.

However, 'training everybody in it' (in this case relevant research) is unlikely to work. That again becomes little more than a top-down programmatic intervention. Transfer of learning will be predictably negligible, because people are not yet grappling with the real questions and issues involved. However, if the context is changed by altering people's roles, relationships and responsibilities around key new tasks, then the felt need to learn by those involved will rise rapidly. For instance, this could be newly empowered teams of multi-agency front-line professionals with their own budgets, and those providing services to them. This is stage three in the critical path to organisational renewal.

Similarly, those leading policy implementation need to understand that they have a problem: that their current state of knowledge is not sufficient for the task. Some know this; many do not, preferring to see the issue as outside themselves. There will be no movement forward until current levels of complacency are interrupted.

Recovery from addiction to failing ways of working

The single biggest danger with the new wave of public service reforms is that those with executive authority for implementation will trigger an unprecedented number of top-down initiatives and projects. These will become ever more time-consuming and complex because of the emphasis on partnership working which will be translated as a series of top-down managing and planning mechanisms. Means will become ends. Process improvement will be detached from outcomes and the focus will go internal. The predominating interest will once again be on inputs and top-down indicators of success. In no time we will have an array of indications that purport to measure the effectiveness of partnerships but that are themselves quite disconnected from the real need for partnership on the ground.

It is simply not possible to produce radically different results by thinking and behaving in the old ways. It is no good directing and expecting others to change and issuing blueprints for homogeneous new cultures. This is little short of madness without a shred of empirical validation. Managers communicate far more through what they are seen to do and how they behave, rather than through what they say, especially in official pronouncements.

Reg Revans talks about the principle of insufficient mandate:

> **... managers who cannot change their predisposing views to their own resistant problems during their efforts to treat those problems will never be able to make progress with them ... managers are themselves necessarily changed in the act of changing what may at first seem to be unchangeable. (Revans, 1982, pp 637-8)**

Programmatic Taylorist approaches offer a means of change that appears to avoid these more personal, challenging and risky aspects of change. A new 'programme' can be produced by experts that will adjust the machine. Or at least that is the hallucinogenic promise. Delivering the new agenda in any meaningful way may well require a little cold turkey first – the withdrawal from old habits.

Perhaps both policy makers and executive implementors should heed the apocryphal teachings and warnings of W. Edward Deming and Reg Revans before rushing headlong into the next frenzied wave of mad management disease. After all, it did a number of Japanese manufacturers no harm. But if you say that producing cars is different – which it is –

remember, that nearly all the tools and techniques you are currently using probably have their origins in manufacturing industries. Further, much of Revans' pioneering action learning work was done in the British public services, but for the most part, remains ignored because it challenged the Taylorist shibboleths of the day – and today.

Taking community involvement seriously

There are two significant issues to be addressed here before clarifying the necessity for involvement, especially in the more distressed localities.

Firstly, while involvement is frequently advocated in official policy documents, it usually represents little more than occasional consultation via surveys, focus groups, citizens' juries or ad hoc community gatherings to comment upon professional and officer agendas and plans. These methods do have their proper place and can be extremely valuable in reviewing service delivery and improvement. They are also the preferred ways of most professionals. Both the means of collection, methods and purposes of analysis, and influence on subsequent decisions and plans (if any) remain firmly within their control. Their orientation is essentially consumerist and there is often nothing wrong with that – except when they purport to be something different, for example, involving and empowering. This is the way that a superficial understanding of the need for involvement is usurped by keeping control within the official 'machine'.

Secondly, there are a number of other concerns that have been expressed about the recent emphasis on geographic community, capacity building, and community involvement for instance; it is idealistic, calling for unreasonable levels of self-sacrificing; it is a throwback to early 1970s notions of self-sufficiency; it is patronising to the poor and disadvantaged; and/or it is simply a way of passing all the responsibility back to impoverished communities in particular and absolving the official agencies for their own failings in fragmented delivery. These are all valuable warnings, and need to be used to continually review and check the purposes for, and the direction of, community involvement.

It is advocated here that community involvement should be taken seriously for a number of linked reasons. These are largely prosaic and based in notions of longer-term enlightened self-interest. But before listing these, *one particular criticism does need addressing*. This is that emphasis is being placed on community of place rather than, or in isolation from, other communities and networks of interest. After all, how many of us put much effort into building our own communities, preferring instead to 'network' in a number of different communities of activity and interest? But, usually we can take a number of things for granted about most, or all, of our neighbours. They do not intimidate us, threaten us or steal from us. If we need some help from them we know that we can depend on it. Even if extremely weak, there is a significant level of background trust and reciprocity. It is a level of social cohesion built upon social capital that we can still depend on. We forget this at our peril.

It is the absence of this geographically-based social capital that is so damaging to people's quality of life, well-being and self-image; when people live in states of continuing anxiety and stress, where trust is low and suspicion is high. Lack of employment, money, and transport has already lessened, or cut off, their links into other communities of interest. Hence, community of place is where the rebuilding has to start as the path of rebuilding networks of trust and the means to build the confidence and personal skills to link into wider networks of *both* community and interest.

In brief, the reasons why community involvement and capacity building are essential in so many neighbourhoods are as follows:

- All the evidence says so.
- Local people know most about local conditions. They can be crucial in both the diagnosis of the systemic causes of problems and who should be engaged in their amelioration. They also know about existing community networks and how to develop these rather than having them ruptured by clumsy top-down interventions. In regeneration projects especially, entry strategies are at least as important as exit strategies.
- It is through the development of local agendas and the active participation of community partnerships that accountability for holistic outcomes can be maintained. Without this, internal silo agendas may usurp them.
- Social capital can only be rebuilt by people themselves taking responsibility for its creation. It is the role of front-line professions to deliver services in concert to assist this.
- It is the central means whereby critical masses of local people own the small improvements that start to make the difference and have a huge stake in their sustainability.
- It acts as the continuing and developing outward focus to meld the best of the various professional knowledges with knowledge of local circumstances and conditions. Professional practice is improved as a result of working closely with those living the journey.
- Well-developed community partnerships and membership

arrangements (including the possibility of local representative democracy) provide for continuity of external outcome focus and lessen the possibility of capture and entryism by unrepresentative voices.

- It is an important stepping stone for many to start connecting beyond the confines and isolation of the local patch.
- It is the most effective way to start connecting with any existing social and civic entrepreneurs, self-help groups and so on, as well as providing fertile ground for promoting the development of these activities.

Getting beyond zero-sum power games and establishing trust

While there is much more recognition of the need to achieve win-win outcomes where there is conflict and/or division, much top management behaviour appears to derive from a deeper assumption that there is only a limited amount of power available to drive and control the organisation (or machine). This corresponds to a similar conception of the limits of available resources. When so much professional activity appears based on deficit models of client and community needs – on what people have not 'got' – this accentuates both lack of power and resources to change. Driven from these perspectives, management becomes more a matter of control, doing what can be done and keeping the lid on any number of impending crises – keeping the machine on track. Such organisations are for ever held on the curative path.

A move towards holistic, preventative, outcome-oriented government is dependent upon involving all those affected across the whole system in the search for improvement. It is about increasing the capacity and competencies to act collaboratively to engage in preventative activity. This necessitates letting go of the desire for tight procedural 'input' controls. It means giving tough direction about overall purposes and outcomes; building on current strengths across agencies and into communities; increasing the power to *act* in order to involve and move towards preventative outcomes, especially at the front-line interface. Without such a shift, empowered front-line multi-agency teams cannot begin to function. Nor can public organisations risk real involvement with those in communities. And this is where the resources lie to redevelop civic community and social capital. Without this, public provision will always be re-diverted back to a virtually exclusive curative agenda. At its core, this new agenda is about rebuilding trust – the social capital of the delivery agencies as well as of communities.

Marvin Weisbord (1987) has illustrated the historical development in organisations from the top-down expert Taylorist solutions to the inclusive, empowering models required for the future.

1900 – experts solve problems
1950 – everybody solves problems
1965 – experts improve whole systems
2000 – everybody improves whole systems.

On Weisbord timelines, some parts of public services have yet to reach 1950.

Best Value: the making or breaking of holistic government

Simply defined, Best Value places an obligation on a local authority to continually search to improve the quality, effectiveness and efficiency of all its activities and service delivery to the public. Local authorities are usually going to be a vital component of locally-based strategies to tackle social exclusion, regeneration and sustainable curative government despite the range of other agencies that are essential to success. Thus, the way in which local authorities approach Best Value is an issue of the utmost importance.

Following the implementation of the government's White Paper on local government, they will be under an obligation to collaborate with other agencies, as well as having an obligation to promote the economic, social and environmental well-being of their area. Further, they will have a duty to consult with local people over service improvements in pursuit of Best Value as well as over the formulation of community plans. This simply adds to the plethora of requirements for consultation, collaboration and partnerships. Best Value should not therefore be seen apart from the full range of public service reforms.

If the predominant focus of Best Value is upon the improvement of individual services, this will inevitably tend to lessen the significance of cross-boundary working. It will lead to a concentration on performance indicators and accountability regimes that reflect the priorities of single services alone. This will make it extremely difficult for multi-agency front-line teams to develop effective collaborative action and involve local communities. Each member will be held accountable for achieving targets by their immediate silo-based superiors. Joined-up action on the ground will be stillborn. There could be no better way of maintaining the status quo. Public service improvement would be rooted in a narrowly focused consumerist agenda which may suit the needs of the prosperous half of the community quite well, but offer little except greater fragmentation of effort elsewhere. Again, it will also inevitably leave the predominant emphasis on cure rather than prevention.

On the other hand, if Best Value is to play a necessary role in promoting holistic, outcome-oriented government, then it must be geared to promoting integrated activity across services through empowered front-line teams. And it is through them that public consultation and involvement should mainly take place, certainly in the more troubled areas.

Of course, all local authorities will employ the language of joined-up rhetoric in approaching Best Value – and their other obligations. Hopefully, the relevant regulatory bodies should have reasonably developed bullshit detectors to unravel this, assuming that they think it is an issue in the first place. If not, we are likely to end up with a mish-mash of confusion, rhetoric and increasing frustration, especially for front-line staff and those in excluded communities. However, as already discussed at the end of Chapter 7 (p 134), the early responses by the Audit Commission are not particularly encouraging, especially from the perspectives taken in this report.

Real change takes time

Invariably, in any given location and context, it has taken many years for current states to be as they are; they are the outcome of complex system dynamics that involve people in communities and a myriad of agencies, institutions and external influences. In all likelihood it will take many years to produce the greatly superior outcomes that can be produced by shifting to greater preventative, quality of life, culture changing focus.

At the same time, appeals for the need for more time will undoubtedly be made by the complacent and those who simply do not want to contemplate change. Therefore, both policy makers and executive implementors need to maintain the pressures for change and create the necessary receptive conditions. At the same time, they have to be as realistic as possible about the time scales required to produce real change through joined-up working on the ground.

A fundamental challenge to current ways of working

These six issues constitute a fundamental challenge to the current workings and cultures of public services, and especially to those services in local government whose lead role will be so vital in the changes that are required.

If they are unwilling or unable to meet these challenges and reconfigure front-line services around local agendas, then (as with local management of schools) it is likely that some combination of legislation will be required to force this together with the development of alternative delivery agencies.

Nor are these issues that will pass with changes of government. The reasons for this are set out in Chapter 1. This and successive governments will be forced to seek more preventative, cost-effective, culture changing solutions to intractable joined-up problems. If public service agencies are unable to adapt to these demands, then it is inevitable that they will be bypassed and disassembled by default. There are equally radical centre-right approaches waiting in the wings. These could reinvent Burke's 'little platoons' and link this to individual initiative, particularly by embracing social and civic entrepreneuralism alongside economic entrepreneuralism.

A paradigm shift

This has been an overused word in recent years, but in the context of the issues raised in this report, and particularly in this chapter, it is probably of some relevance. Sue Richards illustrates significant public policy system shifts in three phases in the grid reproduced as Table 4.

Table 4: Cross-cutting issues in public policy and public service

	Key drivers of public expenditure	Principles of organisational structuring	Form of central control	Mode of policy integration
1945-79	Keynesian demand management – focus on inputs	Professional expertise	Loosely coupled	Organic gradual adjustment
1979-97	'More for less' in public expenditure – focus on throughput	Professional expertise, but with purchaser/ provider split	Tightly coupled and fragmenting	Overloaded and incapable of dealing with fragmented system
1997 - emergent	Effectiveness in public expenditure – focus on outcomes	Problem/task -focused. Process rather than structure	Tight on outcomes/looser on means. Facilitate a learning process	Leadership of cultural change. Incentives for outcomes integration through subsidiarity

Key features of the public policy system in three phases

[Reproduced by permission of Sue Richards]

Her characterisation of the shift to a new emergent post-1997 third phase (way?) provides a coherent framework to illustrate the core paradox involved in leading the implementation of holistic government and governance, especially at local levels. Quite simply, principles of organisational structuring, forms of central control and modes of policy integration will have to change. Past ways of thinking and working can only produce more within the existing paradigm (or phase).

If holistic government is to be implemented it means moving to the new ways of working developed through this report. The six issues that have to be addressed will be at the heart of moving towards Sue Richards' third post-1997 emergent phase. If the old (1979-97) principles of organisational structuring, forms of control and modes of integration remain dominant (and this will need to be much more than just a change of language/rhetoric) then the potential third phase will be temporarily frustrated. In effect, this will result from the vested interests of the many who gain from the current status quo, especially in terms of power and control. On the other hand, the pressures for a radical shift will continue to mount, not least because of pressure on limited public spending to produce more effective outcomes.

Sue Richards' grid provides the macro context for what is struggling to emerge. At the micro level, the Reverend Chris Thorpe describes what can happen when a local authority and its partner agencies do start to cross the threshold into a new paradigm (see Box 12 below). This is a story that sits well alongside those of the many entrepreneurs, social and civic, who have moved into the new emergent phase. But how much more could be achieved if the institutional context could create receptive conditions for learning and change rather than frustrating the efforts of those who are adopting the new ways? And this means moving from rhetoric to reality.

Box 12: Street level democracy in Walsall

"For the past 18 months here in Harden we have been working to implement Walsall's new big idea, the Local Committee.

We have been working out the practical side of this new kind of local democracy, breaking new ground in empowering local people. And for me, as Chair of the Harden Local Committee, these early months have shown that change really is possible, even in areas where many had written us off.

Using a successful Single Regeneration Budget bid, Walsall Council has so far set up seven of these local committees. Representatives are elected on a one-per-hundred-houses basis. You have to live locally and be known locally to get elected.

First meetings: shouting matches!

Our first meetings were angry shouting matches. There has long been a real gap between ordinary people and those who make decisions about them. Local people felt that they had been consulted in the past but then ignored; promises had been made and then broken. No wonder there was scepticism and mistrust at the outset.

No wonder, either, that Harden has experienced the lowest turnouts in the borough for local and national elections. People here felt disregarded, unimportant and completely powerless to influence their future. There was a strong sense of social exclusion, as it has now become popular to term it.

Changes since then: real decisions

In the last year, however, the Local Committee has begun to find its feet and the character of the meetings has changed enormously, building on constructive discussion and decision making. The most important difference in this initiative is that it has placed real decision making in local people's hands.

The SRB funding has meant that our meetings can spend real money: it has given us authority to summon officials and to ensure that we are heard. This provides an amazing opportunity to learn how to work together, how to balance priorities and needs, and to begin to identify the issues that the people of Harden care about.

We have tried from the beginning to hold our meetings at a regular time, in a regular place. Tuesday night is local committee night, with the main committee and different sub-groups meeting month by month in a local church hall.

Community involvement

We have encouraged members of the public to come along to express their views and to play a part in the discussions. So far, the response has been very encouraging. The constant presence of members of the public means that the local committee cannot become remote; and that the people of Harden can participate and influence what goes on.

Here in Harden, we believe that bringing the decisions to the most local level will offer real cost savings in the long run, by getting the answer right first time. It is good to see local people suggesting new solutions to old problems, often surprising the council officers with their insight and imagination.

Council officers working with the local committees need to appreciate that decisions are now made by the local people. From our end, it is easy to spot the officers who have fully embraced and understood this new way of working. They are the ones who do much more than just go through the motions – the ones who understand that the genuine decision makers are the local people.

There are still some important questions that we face as we try to work out how the local committee fits in with other local initiatives. How, for example, should we relate to the community associations, the residents' groups and the potential estates management boards?

Beyond SRB funding

The SRB funding has its limitations: it is only available for five years and it can only be spent on certain defined areas. But perhaps the most exciting aspect of the committee's work is when we have begun to identify problems and situations not covered by the SRB funding. Then it is the mainstream spending that we can influence. One such project is our campaign for a new health centre, inviting doctors and chemists, health authority officials and residents along to meet and talk. When City Challenge and SRB come to an end, this real local democracy has the potential to become part of our long-term future, to change the way we 'do' local government for Harden, for Walsall and beyond.

Consistent respect and authority to local people

In 10 years of involvement with grassroots community development, this is the most positive approach I have encountered. Local committees give real respect and authority to local people.

If we allow local committees to become one more short-term flash-in-the-pan 'programme', then I feel we will have failed the local people and betrayed their trust. However, if we persevere with local committees, so giving consistent respect and authority to local people, then I believe places like Harden can begin to change for good." (The Reverend Chris Thorpe, Vicar of St Aidan's Church and Chair of Harden Local Committee)

NINE

Working in the middle ground: recommendations to promote joined-up action on the ground

"Partnerships, empowering communities, sustainability ... we are doing that already." (Any one of thousands of public service chief executives, directors and service managers [and some politicians])

"Partnerships, empowering communities, sustainability ... we've been elected at the ballot box so we are entitled to tell people what they need. That's why they elected us." (Many of the other local politicians)

Faced with the choice between changing one's mind and proving there is no need to do so, almost everybody gets busy with the proof. (J.K. Galbraith, quoted by Bright, 1997, p 110)

When it comes to contemplating radical change, especially that which requires the embracing of other professional worlds and life in neighbourhoods and communities, much of local government in particular has been a hot bed of complacency. The institutions of local government have been continuously critical of centrally-determined policy for reform directed at it, but have not been able to formulate their own proposals and innovations that address the essential need to reform.

Further, the level of resources devoted to research and development is pitiful. While some other areas of public service may have been a little more innovative, the overall history has been depressing.

Currently, public service agencies are giving considerable attention to the more structural and legalistic aspects of the reform agenda. While this is necessary, it is also entirely predictable that they will do this largely to the exclusion of these aspects that relate more closely to the issues being addressed here. This is simply to follow the Fordist and Taylorist traditions and their preoccupation with the structural aspects of power and control.

Most attention in local government is likely to focus upon deriving new structures and mechanisms of governance and partnership as ends in themselves. Similarly, the reorganisational aspects around the formation of primary care groups – not to mention the political obsession with waiting lists – may well take attention away from the primary purposes of the reforms. For the police service, the immediate legal, structural and partnership aspects of the Crime and Disorder Bill are likely to become paramount. The real concern is that many of our public services will not progress beyond these short-term concerns. What should be the means towards longer-term ends become ends in themselves. Each agency may pursue partnership, consultation and involvement, driven from its own agenda and needs, and the necessity 'to comply' with the formal aspects of government requirements. Government departments are likely to exacerbate this effect with ever lengthening notes of guidance and instruction, largely the result of people telling others how to do what they have never done themselves. Indeed, there are very few existing models or examples of how to do it, apart from the empirical studies of valiant activity of people 'on the ground', frequently having to work against the tide of prevailing conformity.

The worst scenario across many districts will be the development of a plethora of disjointed 'partnership' activity absorbing huge amounts of top management time and attention. This will be accompanied by endless disconnected consultation and participation exercises designed around the short term and different needs of the agencies, rather than around the needs of people in local neighbourhoods. The more this happens, the more it will kill existing social and civic entrepreneurship and local community capacity building, let alone create the conditions for joined-up action on the ground.

The job of executive implementors at the local level is to create, through genuine engagement between themselves, the conditions and mechanisms for effective neighbourhood level partnership working.

The recommendations that follow are designed to promote this and work against the endemic preoccupation with these central and corporate issues that can become dangerously disconnected from the intentions of the reforms. Their purpose is to put attention and resourcing into the gap and spaces that are largely ignored:

• between people in local communities;

- between communities and neighbourhoods themselves;
- between the agencies enabling them to become better partners with citizens and local communities;
- between the agencies and citizens/communities.

This new focus on the 'middle ground' – the gap between 'bottom-up' and 'top-down' and the horizontal divisions between communities and between agencies – is designed to ensure that the progressive transformation of the public services is formed on holistic outcomes for citizens and communities, *as expressed by them*. There is a high requirement for this reconnection. Sadly, the resources of time and money are locked up *within* current institutional cultural and control systems. New seed resources, together with incentives and penalties, need to change this by rewarding collaborative activity and *learning through action* to overcome this endemic tendency.

There has always been much frustrated energy for innovation in the public services. Charles Leadbeater's identification of civic entrepreneurialism is a manifestation of this. It is also clear that the government's reforms and proposals have triggered a wave of interest and enthusiasm for change and a welcome recognition that things need to be done very differently. These are the essential sparks capable of igniting a new culture of learning derived out of action – of tackling key issues on the ground. What is now required is a range of 'light' policy interventions, incentives and penalties that will:

- Encourage countervailing forces that are designed to develop and facilitate local voice of both communities and many of the front-line workers who recognise the need for change. This seeks to overcome the disconnections between the political, professional and managerial worlds on the one hand, and so much of local community on the other; the meeting ground between top-down and bottom-up.
- Provide the means and support for new forms of collaborative working where people across the whole system can build their own visions and design action to which they are all committed. The best implementation *always* comes from self-motivated and committed people. Complementary action when partners are apart produces joined-up action, not a superficial teaminess when they are together.
- Interrupt the status quo, where for instance regulatory bodies in particular will need to have sufficiently well-established bullshit detectors (measures of soft and hard holistic outcomes) to challenge and expose rhetoric/reality gaps where they appear.

- Promote the development of empowered front-line multi-agency teams with devolved budgets working towards the achievement of holistic outcomes based upon locally-determined definitions of need and quality of life improvement.
- Focus research and development activity on whole system and action learning processes that specifically cut across current disconnections, especially between agencies and communities.

Developing 'middle ground' activity

Government and the newly emerging Regional Development Agencies (RDAs) in particular, should actively promote and encourage minimalist and facilitative projects such as C2M in Bradford and similar projects that are emerging elsewhere. Their roles would cover some or all of the following:

- stimulating community and neighbourhood-based audit, planning and action;
- connecting existing and emerging community activists, energisers and social entrepreneurs with each other and across counties and districts;
- enabling agencies to become better partners with communities (and by implication with each other).

Such bodies need to engage with, and seek the cooperation of, the key stakeholders in a district but have their own independent basis of existence. Their function *would not be* one of coordination, nor to do what other bodies are already doing, or in the longer term, should be doing. They should therefore have a finite life span of up to, say, seven years.

National Lottery and other relevant funding regimes would need to promote innovation in the creation of these activities.

Adjusting regeneration funding regimes

Funding regimes and monitoring mechanisms should be adjusted to provide two broad categories of support.

- There should be a far greater use of smaller grants (say £50,000–£500,000) to help to 'stabilise' fractured communities, especially where levels of criminality, intimidation and destructive damage is high. There are particularly important roles here for local housing management and police, working with other agencies on the ground. In the worst cases such stabilisation work will need to be done before it is reasonable to elicit much local support or enthusiasm. Applications should come from local agencies starting to work together as partners around communities. These types of bids should also clarify:

- how local people are being supported to undertake audit and planning of local need and existing capacity (avoiding starting with a deficit perspective);
- steps to be taken towards creating local community planning processes which are rooted in the local definitions of need;
- support from agency headquarters showing how the proposals mesh with their overall strategies; in the cases of social housing landlords and police authorities, it would be important to link this to strategies for improving locally-based community responsiveness;
- how local services are to be reconfigured around neighbourhoods and their agendas (see below).

• Larger awards should normally only be granted when the local conditions above are clearly established as the foundation. Capacity building and real community-based partnership planning should be at their core. Wherever possible, communities themselves should be encouraged to take a key role in leading local partnership with the statutory bodies and other stakeholders as key partners. Communities should be in a position to 'contest' the delivery of regeneration projects.

It would be realistic to expect most local delivery agencies to be involved in bids, explaining how they are going to work together and with their communities to address local needs and problems. Local authorities and other sponsoring bodies should provide staff support to facilitate and work up the programmes, but ownership and authorship must rest in the community and with local delivery. Typically this should involve schools, health centres, GPs, police, social workers, youth work, primary care staff, local housing management, cleansing and grounds maintenance and so on. Capital spending in particular, should be appraised for complementary and joint use. This should apply equally to 'mainstream' funds.

RDAs would have a particular responsibility for ensuring that project appraisal systems are designed to ensure that projects deliver sustainable holistic outcomes, linked to improving quality of life.

There is a real danger that New Deal for Communities, by

concentrating large amounts of money on a very limited number of small neighbourhoods, will divert attention away from the vital elements of reconfiguration. A very much larger number of far smaller grants could act as a catalyst for this new joining-up between front-line service delivery and re-emerging communities. This is central to a number of proposals being made by Dick Atkinson in his forthcoming Demos publication which have particular relevance here.

Developing empowered multi-agency front-line teams

Getting better value from mainstream spending lies at the core of modernising public services. It is clear that the way to do this is through their reconfiguration around neighbourhood agendas. This should not be seen as just a component of regeneration projects. It should be applied much more widely to include areas that do not fit official definitions of deprivation (in any case, as much deprivation exists in areas that *do not* themselves fall under the definition of deprivation, as in those that *do*).

Appropriately reconfigured local teams need to be able to work towards the achievement of shared visions and plans for improvement with local agendas. This will require moving towards pooled budgets and having a neighbourhood team leader. (A discussion document from the Department of Health, 1998, offers some welcome early pointers here.) The development of such teams will mean fundamentally altering the relationships between front-line professionals and back-line management, organisation and services in the way that devolved budgets and management has done in schools. Front-line teams could then be held accountable for the achievement of holistic outcomes tied to the sustainable improvement in quality of life for people who live in the patch. They would also act as mediators for developing back-line *public service contracts* (service level agreements) between back-line providers and the communities themselves.

Local government will need to take the main lead in this. As with the delegation of school budgets, many are likely to be highly resistant to this and their perceived lack of control. Government will need to devise a series of incentives and penalties to ensure that this happens. They should also consider experimentation with alternative forms of provision through third sector and private provision, particularly favouring social entrepreneurs, the development of tenant management and ownership schemes, the formation of development trusts and so on. They should also encourage experiments in neighbourhood democracy similar to those being pioneered in Walsall.

In the long run they may have to develop legislation to create this. But much should be achieved through regulation of measures already in place and being developed. Of particular importance here are Best Value, beacon status, partnerships between health and social services, the action zones, the development of *real* local planning, and the direction *and application* of future regeneration funding regimes (see above). The need for the development of sufficiently robust detectors to challenge and expose rhetoric/reality gaps will be essential.

In short, the development of empowered multi-agency front-line teams will need[1]

• to be at the core of improving the value of mainstream service delivery and not as a component of 'regeneration';
• pooled budgets and designated team leaders;
• to be accountable for holistic outcomes resulting in the sustained improvement of the quality of life for local people as perceived by them;
• to act as intermediaries in the development of *public service contracts* (or Local Performance Plans, LPPs) between back-line services and local people, perhaps through locally elected committees;
• experimentation with alternative forms of provision, especially through the third sector to encourage development trusts, tenant management and ownership schemes, and social entrepreneuralism;
• a regime of government incentives, penalties and regulations (and as a fall back, legislation) to overcome likely institutional resistance.

Sponsoring action research, development and learning

This has been an area of chronic neglect. There needs to be a national initiative and new agency set up to promote this. Currently, public sector organisations and their representative bodies can only contract for research and development work within the predominantly Fordist and Taylorist paradigms with which they are familiar. Current arrangements for funding development, especially in health and local government, are likely to increase the tendency for promoting detached rhetoric while sponsoring silo-focused development.

A Public Service Development Board (PSDB) needs to be established that can promote and fund research and development work based upon the following.

- Change processes that work and that are geared to addressing the achievement of holistic preventative outcomes.
- The dissemination of good practice and research evidence.
- Confronting the six key issues that have to be addressed if holistic, prevention-oriented government is to become a reality:
  - developing evidence-based approaches to change – using the research;
  - recovery from addiction to failing ways of working;
  - taking community involvement seriously;
  - getting beyond zero-sum power games and establishing trust;
  - Best Value; the making or breaking of holistic government;
  - real change takes time.
- Action learning and whole system projects that are grounded in real change activity, rather than restructuring, training and attending conferences.

The PSDB would work at three levels of hierarchy.

Firstly, a small national centre (there should be separate bodies to cover England, Wales, Scotland and Northern Ireland) responsible for setting the directions, reviewing progress and consolidating and disseminating learning. It would have particular roles in relating to appropriate government departments and agencies especially those promoting lateral working, and to regulatory functions.

The PSDB also needs to research, develop and promote new career pathways that reward both social and civic entrepreneurial behaviours. For the most part, these are not characteristics that have been sufficiently recognised or rewarded in the past.

Secondly, regional centres which would be closely linked with, or be part of, the RDAs. Apart from directly sponsoring and commissioning work at the local levels, they would promote networks of research and development, innovation, and learning across their regions. These would include activity in local communities, across districts as well as between delivery agencies themselves and their communities.

This could fit alongside the role of RDAs as animateurs in the development of endogenous regeneration policies that feature the building of trust, learning and social capital (see especially Cooke and Morgan, 1998).

Thirdly, local development sites that would be set up by collaboration between public service agencies and stakeholder partners, and part-funded by them to match PSDB funding. Their primary purpose would be to promote action and whole system learning across their wider systems to stimulate and accelerate implementation of joined-up action on the ground.

Social housing policy

Although there has been little direct mention of housing policy in this report, all the evidence shows that active, intensive, sensitive local management, with high levels of tenant involvement, is vital to improving the quality of life on the worst estates. Although decentralisation through housing associations, and various tenant management schemes has been promoted by previous governments, the impact of CCT tended to work in opposition to this. Every opportunity must be sought to promote decentralised housing management including tenant participation in the *management of the locality as a whole*.

The recommendations made by Michael Young and Gerard Lemos should also be pursued:

- Building communities should, along with meeting housing need, be a central policy purpose of social housing.
- Social housing should be allocated according to social as well as housing needs. Mutuality points could be transferred from people needing support to those willing to give it.
- All social landlords should be required to incorporate social needs in allocations and encourage mutual aid between tenants and neighbours by offering the Mutual Aid Compact to all new tenants.
- Some of the available capital receipts should be given over to the employment of community development coordinators by housing associations, local authorities and voluntary bodies to promote and develop mutual aid in their neighbourhoods.
- Social landlords should encourage mutual aid. This would mean providing more new social housing for three generations with a mutualist approach to housing and estate management. It would mean encouraging local job creation and organising social care locally for children and elderly and disabled people, provided by volunteers as well as paid professionals. A Mutual Aid Housing Advisory Centre could assist and enable social landlords to develop informal and formal mutual aid by giving them advice and encouragement.
- In areas of mixed tenure housing, churches and other local voluntary bodies should undertake community audits to bring together those in need of support with those volunteers willing to give it. Local authorities should incorporate the findings of the community audits into the proposed community plans.

The integration, coordination and simplification of planning systems

The White Paper (*Modern local government: In touch with the people*) proposals promoting the well-being of communities are very much to be welcomed. These include a new duty to promote economic, social and environmental well-being as well as the need to attain greater cohesion and coherence at local levels through community planning.

It is very much to be hoped that this community planning is both sufficiently locally based (at the levels of developing local communities) and involving to address the issues raised in this report. Plans must be developed out of local need and ownership, otherwise they will inevitably revert to being ends rather than means, being produced for the sole purpose of satisfying top-down demands.

Further, these planning processes need to link both 'hard' and 'soft' infrastructures. This needs to be done in two ways, horizontally and vertically. The building block for these should be neighbourhood-based community plans.

Horizontal integration: government at all levels plans transport, economic regeneration, housing, health, education, leisure and sport, waste collection and disposal and so on – all within a planned capital and revenue budget. All are done within different legal frameworks to different time scales, by different agencies. There needs to be progress towards integrating these, echoing nationally what was effectively done when new towns were created. There also needs to be a coherent set of Planning Policy Guidelines (PPGs) that reflect this integration, together with the imperatives of sustainability, involvement, capacity building and neighbourhood plans.

Vertical integration: RDAs need to promote within their framework plans the development of iterative linkages connecting regional, district (local authority), and neighbourhood planning processes.

Increasing the focus on prevention

There needs to be protection, and the progressive increase of activities, budgets, professional development and career pathways that favour prevention through the tackling of systemic causation.

Beacon councils

Beacon status should only be awarded to those public bodies that can demonstrate their active reconnection to local communities through genuine multi-agency partnership leading to the attainment of holistic outcomes.

Conclusion

This report has attempted to analyse, from the perspectives of research findings and our own practice, the barriers to joined-up action on the ground and to make suggestions about which actions might create the right conditions for helpful change. Inevitably, in trying to analyse and identify problems and challenges, it may appear as if we are attempting to lay blame at the door of certain institutions.

Since the mid-1970s, our society has been coping with rapid economic, technological, political and social change. We are all living in a different sort of world where the frameworks which served us for more than 30 years are no longer useful. The institutions, agencies and services in all sectors – private, public and voluntary – are all having to reinvent themselves. Communities, in terms of what they look like and how they understand themselves, have also undergone significant changes in response. In these circumstances a culture of blame is unhelpful and misplaced.

As we have discussed the contents of this report with individuals and groups, as well as during the development of C2M and work in Walsall, it has been exhilarating to discover how many people do share at least the broad analysis and have identified the same issues which need to be addressed. This is what makes the moment so opportune. However, it is one thing to believe that change needs to come and quite another to be confident or gain agreement about how to implement it. Uncertainty and a lack of knowledge about what might be possible makes more urgent the need to disseminate useful examples of good practice. Examples which tell the whole story including the difficult parts. Successful working usually develops out of previous acknowledged and evaluated 'failures'.

At the beginning of this report, in the Acknowledgements, we wrote that our intention in producing this report was to influence policy. If the two key messages of this report – about the urgent need to create the receptive conditions for institutional change and development and the need to act on the belief that communities can be architects of their own futures – eventually become reflected in public policy then we will be content.

Note

[1] These proposals are somewhat similar to those being put forward by Dick Atkinson in his forthcoming *The third way: From welfare state to welfare society*, to be published by Demos.

References

Appelbee, E. (1998) 'Keys to learning', Keynote address to the North of England Education Conference, Bradford, 5-7 January.

Argyris, C. and Schon, D.A. (1978) *Organisational learning: A theory of action perspective*, Reading, MA: Addison Wesley.

Atkinson, D. (1994) *The common sense of community*, London: Demos.

Atkinson, D. (forthcoming) *The third way: From welfare state to welfare society*, London: Demos.

Audit Commission (1998) *Better by far – preparing for Best Value*, Best Value Management Paper 1, December, London [Vincent Square, SW1P 2PN].

Bateson, G. (1972) *Steps to an ecology of mind*, San Francisco, CA: Aronson.

Beer, M., Eisenstat, R.A. and Spector, B. (1990) *The critical path to corporate renewal*, Boston, MA: Harvard Business School Press.

Bright, J. (1997) *Turning the tide: Crime, community and prevention*, London: Demos.

Carers National Association (1998) *Ignored and invisible: Carers' experience of the NHS*, London: Carers National Association, Tel 0171 490 8818.

Clark, T.N. (1997) *The new political culture*, Boulder, Co: Westview Press.

Clark, T.N. and Rempel, M. (1997) *Citizen policies in post-industrial societies*, London: Harper Collins.

Cohen, J. and Arato, A. (1992) *Civil society and political theory*, Boston, MA: MIT Press.

Cooke, P. and Morgan, K. (1998) *The associational economy – firms, regions and innovation*, Oxford: Oxford University Press.

Corrigan, P. and Joyce, P. (1997) 'Reconstructing public management: a new responsibility for the public and a case study of local government', *International Journal of Public Sector Management*, vol 10, no 6, pp 417-32.

DETR (Department of the Environment, Transport and the Regions) (1997) *Regeneration programmes: The way forward*, Discussion Paper, London: DETR.

DETR (1998a) *Modern local government: In touch with the people*, Cm 4014, July, London: The Stationery Office.

DETR (1998b) *Sustainable local communities of the 21st century*, London: DETR.

Deming, W.E. (1986) *Out of crisis*, Cambridge: Cambridge University Press.

Democratic Renewal Debate, DETR (1998) *Modernising local government: Local democracy and community leadership*, Consultation Paper, London and Middlesex: DETR and Publication Sales Unit.

Dixon, N. (1994) *The organizational learning cycle: How we can learn collectively*, Maidenhead: McGraw-Hill.

DoE (Department of the Environment) (1972) *The new local authorities: Management and structures*, The Baines Report, London.

DoE (1995) *Involving communities in urban and rural regeneration: A guide for practitioners*, November, London: DoE.

DoH (Department of Health) (1998) *Partnership in health and social services*, Discussion document, September.

Drath, W. and Palus, C. (1994) *Making common sense: Leadership as meaning making in a community of practice*, Greensboro, NC: Center for Creative Leadership.

Ferlie, E., Ashburner, L., Fitzgerald, L. and Pettigrew, A. (1996) *The new public management in action*, Oxford: Oxford University Press.

Fordham, G. (1995) *Made to last: Creating sustainable neighbourhood and estate regeneration*, York: Joseph Rowntree Foundation.

Forster, E.M. (1910) 'Epigraph', *Howards End*, London: Penguin.

Fullan, M. (1991) *The new meaning of educational change*, London: Cassell.

Garratt, B. (ed) (1995) *Developing strategic thought: Rediscovering the art of direction giving*, Maidenhead: McGraw-Hill.

Gavron, N. (1998a) 'A better Britain: Planning for sustainable communities: Integration, decentralisation and democracy', Unpublished speech to the RIPI Planning Officers Society Conference, 16 January.

Gavron, N. (1998b) 'New ways forward for planning committees', *Housing and Planning Review*, December/January, pp 23-6.

de Geus, A. (1988) 'Planning as learning', *Harvard Business Review*, March–April, pp 70-4.

de Geus, A. (1997) *The living company: Growth, learning and longevity in business*, London: Nicholas Brearley.

Giddens, A. (1998) *The third way*, London: Polity Press.

Hall, D. (1997a) 'Citizens take control', *Local Government Chronicle*, 7 November, p 15.

Hall, D. (1997b) 'Progress in partnership', *Local Government Chronicle*, 14 November, pp 16-17.

Hall, D. (1997c) 'Bridges to better government', *Local Government Chronicle*, 28 November, p 19.

Hall, D. (1997d) 'Management revamp', *Local Government Chronicle*, 5 December, p 12.

Ham, C. (1996) *Public, private or community: What next for the NHS?*, London: Demos.

Hamel, G. and Prahalad, C. (1989) 'Strategic intent', *Harvard Business Review*, May-June, no 3, pp 63-76.

Hamel, G. and Prahalad, C. (1994) *Competing for the future*, Harvard: Harvard Business School Press.

Hampden-Turner, C. and Trompenaars, F. (1993) *The seven cultures of capitalism*, London: Piatkus.

Hopkins, D., Ainscow, M. and West, M. (1994) *School improvement in an era of change*, London: Cassell.

Heckscher, C. (1995) *White collar blues*, New York, NY: Basic Books.

Heifetz, R.A. (1994) *Leadership without easy answers*, Cambridge, MA: Belknap Press.

Heifetz, R.A. and Laurie, D.L. (1997) 'The work of leadership', *Harvard Business Review*, January–February, pp 124-34.

Hugill, B. (1998) 'Doing the coin street flip', *The Observer*, 7 June.

Kellner, P. (1998) 'A new "ism" for our times', *New Statesman*, 22 May, pp 30-2.

Kennedy, C. and Harvey, D. (1997) *Managing and sustaining radical change*, London: Business Intelligence.

Knight, B. and Stokes, P. (1996) *The deficit in civil society in the United Kingdom*, Working Paper No 1, Birmingham: Foundation for Civil Society, [200 Banbury Road, Northfield, Birmingham B1 2DL].

Knight, B. and Stokes, P. (nd) *Organising a civil society*, Working Paper No 2, Birmingham: Foundation for Civil Society.

Landry, C. and Bianchini, F. (1995) *The creative city*, London: Demos.

Leadbeater, C. (1997) *The rise of the social entrepreneur*, London: Demos.

Leadbeater, C. and Goss, S. (1998) *Civic entrepreneurship*, London: Demos.

LGA (Local Government Association) (1998) *The new commitment to regeneration*, Circular 226/98, 2 April.

McArthur, A. (1995) 'The active involvement of local residents in strategic community partnerships', *Policy & Politics*, vol 23, no 1, pp 61-71 [quoted in Taylor, 1995].

McGonigle, M. (1989) 'Designing for sustainability: a native/ environmentalist perspective for third level government', *BG Studies 84*, pp 65-99.

Mintzberg, H. (1994) *The rise and fall of strategic planning*, Hemel Hempstead: Prentice-Hall.

Mollison, W. (1990) *Permaculture: A practical guide for a sustainable future*, Washington, DC: Island Press.

Morgan, G. (1986) *Images of organisations*, London: Sage.

Mulgan, G. (1997) *Connexity – How to live in a connected world*, London: Chatto & Windus.

Mulgan, G. and Landry, C. (1995) *The other invisible hand: Remaking charity for the 21st century*, London: Demos.

Mulgan, G. and 6, P (1996) 'The local's coming home: decentralisation by degrees', *Demos Quarterly*, Issue 9, pp 3-7.

Murray, R. (1991) 'The state after Henry', *Marxism Today*, May, pp 22-7.

NEF (New Economics Foundation) (1998) *Participation works! 21 techniques of community participation for the 21st century*, London: NEF [1st Floor Vine Court, 112-116 Whitechapel Road, London E1 1JE].

NEF (nd) *Community works. A guide to community economic action*, London: NEF.

Pascale, R. (1990) *Managing on the edge: How successful companies use conflict to stay ahead*, Harmondsworth: Penguin Books.

Pedler, M. (forthcoming) *Action learning for managers*, London: Lemos & Crane.

Pedler, M. (1998) 'Including the excluded, a case study of action learning and whole system development in Walsall', Unpublished article.

Pettigrew, A., Ferlie, E. and McKee, L. (1992) *Shaping strategic change*, London: Sage.

Power, A. (1994) *Area-based poverty, social problems and resident empowerment*, Discussion Paper WSP/107, London: Suntory-Toyota International Centre for Economics and Related Disciplines, London School of Economics.

Power, A. (1997) *Estates on the edge: The social consequences of mass housing in Northern Europe*, Basingstoke: Macmillan.

Power, A. and Tunstall, R. (1995) *Swimming against the tide: Polarisation or progress on 20 unpopular council estates 1980-1995*, York: Joseph Rowntree Foundation.

Putnam, R. (1993) *Making democracy work: Civic traditions in modern Italy*, Princeton, NJ: Princeton University Press.

Rallings, C. and Thrasher, M. (1996) *Enhancing local election turnout*, York: Joseph Rowntree Foundation.

Revans, R. (1982) *The origins and growth of action learning*, Bromley: Chartwell-Bratt.

Revans, R. (1998) *ABC of action learning – empowering managers to act and to learn from action*, The Mike Pedler Library, London: Lemos & Crane.

RSA (1998) *To boldly go: The voluntary sector and voluntary action in the new world of work*, London: RSA.

6, P (1997) *Holistic government*, London: Demos.

Schon, D.A. (1971) *Beyond the stable state*, New York: Random House.

Seddon, J. (1997) *In pursuit of reality – The case against ISO9000*, Dublin: Oak Tree Press.

Senge, P. (1990) *The fifth discipline – The art and practice of the learning organisation*, London: Century Press.

Skinner, S. (1997) *Building community strengths: A resource book on capacity building*, London: Community Development Foundation [60 Highbury Grove, London N5 2AG].

Social Exclusion Unit (1998) *Bringing Britain together: A national strategy for neighbourhood renewal*, Cm 4045, London: HMSO.

Taylor, M. (1995) *Unleashing the potential: Bringing residents to the centre of regeneration*, York: Joseph Rowntree Foundation.

Travers, T. and Jones, G. (1998) 'Tap into the benefits of self-control system', *Local Government Chronicle*, 3 April, p 16.

UNCED (1992) *Agenda 21*, New York: UNCED, United Nations General Assembly.

Weisbord, M. (1987) *Productive workplaces: Organizing and managing for dignity, meaning and community*, San Francisco, CA: Jossey-Bass.

Weisbord, M. (1992) *Discovering common ground: How future search conferences bring people together to achieve breakthrough innovation, empowerment, shared vision and collaborative action*, San Francisco, CA: Berrett-Koehler.

Wilkinson, D. (1997a) 'Whole system development: rethinking public service management', *International Journal of Public Sector Management*, vol 10, no 7, pp 505-33.

Wilkinson, D. (1997b) Unpublished final report of Whole System Development consultancy project on Walsall's SRB.

Wilkinson, D., Attwood, M. and Pedler, M. (1999: forthcoming) *Whole system development*, London: Lemos & Crane.

Wilkinson, D. and Pedler, M. (1996) 'Whole systems development in public service', *The Journal of Management Development*, vol 15, no 2, pp 38-53.

Wilson, W. (1996) 'Are ghettos emerging in Europe?', LSE Housing Workshop, 23-27 June.

Womack, J., Jones, D. and Roos, D. (1990) *The machine that changed the world*, New York: Rawson Associates, McMillan Publishing Company.

World Commission on Environment and Development (1987) *Our common future*, Brundtland Report, Oxford: Oxford University Press.

Young, K. and Rao, N. (1994) *Coming to terms with change? The local government councillor in 1993*, York: Joseph Rowntree Foundation.

Young, M. and Lemos, G. (1997) *The communities we have lost and can regain*, London: Lemos & Crane.

Zimmock, M. (1998) [member of the RSA's Redefining Work team] 'All in good working order', *The Guardian*, 10 June.